SALAD DAYS

T.D. SMART

FOR OGs EVERYWHERE
REAL, IMAGINED OR ASPIRANT

Highbrow option

'My salad days
When I was green in judgment, cold in blood
To say as I said then!'

William Shakespeare, 'Antony and Cleopatra'

Less highbrow option

'These are my salad days
Slowly being eaten away.'

Spandau Ballet, 'Gold'

PART ONE –
PAISLEY, POLITICS,
AND CRICKET

Chapter 1 – Boredom

'It's not important for you to know my name.
Nor I to know yours.
If we communicate for two minutes only.
It will be enough.'

Paul Weller – Start

So, it had come to this: how close – and at what angle – the black 8 ball was to the striped yellow 9 ball. And all because of one inappropriate and drink-inspired comment on a Croatian beach the previous summer. This woman, who he thought had loved him unconditionally for nearly 25 years, was staring at his bound and gagged form, pointing a loaded crossbow between his eyes. Her brown eyes were now all but black. Could it have been different?

This has nothing at all to do with this book, but I am told that the first few sentences are all that can sometimes matter - especially if the writer is a nobody. After that you – the reader – are hopefully hooked. If unsuccessful, you are off to pursue some other activity – forever oblivious to the riches that follow.

Sadly, the real start to this book is boredom, which is apparently not a great seller. No matter how history may spin a 'Dunkirk spirit' kind of vibe, the coronavirus lockdown in Scotland in the spring and early summer of 2020 was really, really boring.

The few things we were allowed to do - read, walk around the block, watch TV – started as some relief, but then became the reinforcing symbols of our captivity. The availability of copious amounts of drink curiously did not lose its appeal; neither did eating lots of shite. But after the eight-week mark, it became increasingly clear that this had the potential for negative consequences.

Self-employed, I had no work. My wife did and was very busy. I sulked about the house like a sorry and self-indulgent teenager. Being a 'kept man' was something I could get used to, but this offered scant comfort for my general disillusionment.

Virtual Zoom pub nights with pals helped, but after a while it became apparent that the instinctive opening line of 'What's been happening?' had become the most redundant phrase in the English language.

I did become very proficient in an online pool game, which offered some diversion. But I had finally to accept my wife's observation that this was keeping me in bed most days till early afternoon and was probably impacting adversely on my mental health. Unlike the Italians, we did not even get access to free TV porn, and taking the bins out became a daily treat.

I then tried to bait some Tories on social media about their government's catastrophic handling of the Covid crisis. But this just made me angry. Although apparently there are lots of them, I discovered that Tories are very good at hiding, not great with numbers, or 'not actually interested in politics.' Landing us with party boy Boris Johnson was apparently a 'non-political' act.

I determined to extend my cooking range. But despite ambition and no little enthusiasm, every dish I started tended to end up as Spaghetti Bolognese. Even I had to accept the constant feedback that I had 'tried hard' was not unambiguously positive, and that Rick Stein was probably safe for now.

To lift my mood, I wrote a more upbeat piece and shared it with friends on social media: '10 things I am most looking forward to doing when the world starts again'. Football, sit-in curries, going to the seaside, seeing friends and family, the pub, the cinema, a Greek island, were all very nice – but hardly controversial. One item, however, generated much more feedback than any of the others: watching cricket.

A simple statement perhaps explains this – I am Scottish, and I live in Glasgow.

Comments flooded back.

'You OK, Tommy?'

'Great gag about the cricket!'

'Number 10 – typo?'

'Always thought you were a bit of a wanker.'

'Great list, I guess you couldn't think of a tenth option.'

'I agree that St. Mirren will probably win the Scottish Premiership next year.'

The first 5 of these are quite representative of the feedback: the last is just made up.

It got me thinking.

Born next to a cricket field, in my early years a love of - and obsession with - cricket seemed a natural thing in my life. The ground was where everything happened – football all the time, cricket in the summer, tennis for two weeks in late June, golf when not hunted by the groundsman. I could not distinguish any particular sporting hierarchy. In the small world of youth, all my friends and neighbours just played everything.

Only as my life expanded did the apparent freakishness of cricket as a Paisley pastime reveal itself. As my horizons grew wider, this sense of participating in some obscure, cultish behaviour intensified. And in the west of Scotland, perceptions of cricket also crossed two very thick red lines – it was 'English', and it was played by toffs!

But my by now established addiction withstood all these attacks. For me, cricket was just too good to abandon, irrespective of the shame it brought on me and my family. Fortunately, my parents stood by me, and some counselling helped. The great game was my first 'habit', for which I have never received effective treatment.

As I entered my later teens, I then discovered an underworld of fellow addicts, even in the mean streets of my home town of Paisley. In secret basement meetings, disguised and hidden from society, we shared our love of great test matches of the past, the smell of linseed oil, and the intoxication of the first cut of grass as a precursor to a new season.

I then went back to my post coronavirus wish list and realised I did not just miss watching cricket, I missed playing it. This could not actually go on my list, as I had long given up participating in my mid-40s. Many people happily play on well beyond this age - as these chronicles testify - but my beloved club had folded, and my 'whites' (essential cricket costume) had not survived a house move.

I did not just miss the actual game, I missed everything that went on around it. I realised I had probably never laughed as much and so consistently as in my time with the Old Grammarians Cricket Club – the OGs. I looked back on endless summer days, freezing dressing rooms, and of feeling a heavy woollen jumper soaked in the Scottish rain whilst desperately pleading for the umpires to shout 'enough'. Truly my 'salad days'.

Most of all, I missed my teammates and the never-ending stream of eccentric characters that populated over twenty years of action.

I cannot know for sure if there is something about cricket that particularly attracts these types –

but I suspect there is. I think it has to do with the long and slow nature of the game, occasionally played in lazy sunshine, and the amount of time you spend together over a few short summer months. I also think the 'sound' of cricket appeals to people with a more 'off centred' view of the world - generally quiet, gentle and reassuring, punctuated with intermittent and often feverish screeches. Although I have never quite been able to define why, I think cricket is inherently comic.

I have always loved books, and like many, intended to write one 'someday'. I felt that day had probably gone, but in an unusual moment of proactivity I joined a creative writing evening class before Christmas 2019. It was great fun, but it did not trigger me to write anything of my own. I knew I was OK at putting words together, doing this for over 30 years in a work context. But I simply couldn't think of anything to write about.

Week 12 of the lockdown: 'To be honest, I'm bored out my tits,' I confided for the 110th time to my wife. After just the two of us for all this time, even her easy-going patience was being stretched.

'You know your problem, don't you?'

After many years of marriage, this opening gambit had the scope to go in many directions. I looked up with some trepidation.

'I was on a virtual Human Resources conference yesterday, and they called you out perfectly.'

'Oh dear,' I thought. 'Had the people trumpeting the wonders of Covid for online learning really thought it all through?'

'MALE, PALE AND STALE!' she announced triumphantly. 'You and your type *are* the problem!'

Now, I have always had two potential options to these not infrequent confrontations. Firstly, to come out fighting, normally led by a devastating, 'What a pile of shite.' But today, in my lugubrious state, I took option two – a childlike, self-pitying huff. It is normally a more productive tactic, and again it worked. Attempting some form of constructive rapprochement, my wife said in softer exasperation:

'Why don't you write something?'

'I've no new ideas. *The Great Gatsby*'s been written.'

This had been my glib and infuriating excuse for years. Scott Fitzgerald's 1925 classic is my favourite book; flawless in my opinion. Who was I to attempt to bat on the same pitch?

My wife continued, 'So nobody else has written anything good for nearly 100 years since?'

I have never liked such damningly accurate statements that undermine my position.

'Remember that post you sent, about all the things you wanted to do after the lockdown, and how astonished you were at the hostile reaction to watching cricket?'

'Philistines! They just don't get it.'

'So why don't you try to write a book that explains it?'

Checkmate.

So in late May 2020, the stars aligned. I had my idea, I had my challenge, and I still had hee-haw else to do. Especially as the coronavirus turned out to be a bit more determined and difficult to dislodge than many English batting lineups.

The idea of writing also worked for me because, like many, the 2020 lockdown was a uniquely reflective time; and at a certain age looking back becomes a richer seam than looking forward. If not quite yet in the autumn of my days, I have to admit the summer nights are getting a bit chillier. Coronavirus also meant that looking forward was frankly depressing. I then remembered an observation about the concept of a 'golden age' in history which cynically suggested that, no matter where you started from, the 'golden age' was always about 30 years earlier. As I thought of my cricket playing days, these timelines just about worked.

So here is my humble offering. Of course it's a book about cricket; but this provides the setting, not the story. Ultimately it is about the characters that play it, the game's absurdities, and the many bizarre situations a life with the OGs gifted. It is also about my home town of Paisley and the west of Scotland, politics, and a little about another of my obsessions - books.

It is an alternative view of friendship – one that suggests you do not always have to admire all the characteristics of a friend. Often it is actually their weaknesses and eccentricities that most matter. This generates a strange type of respect.

As you will become quickly aware, at one level many of my teammates do not come out of these tales well. Morally, some of the behaviour detailed would not pass most acceptable standards. But there is not a single OG mentioned that I did not ultimately like. My life would have been the poorer for never knowing them.

Are these memoirs factually accurate? On balance, not really. Some things are without doubt true: there was a cricket team called the OGs, there is a Paisley Grammar School, Scottish summers can be unreliable, and incredibly, there does exist a wee man called Jacob 'Money Can't Buy Me Brains' Rees-Mogg. Many of the OG characters depicted are loosely based on real people, but somewhat exaggerated. Strangely, some of the most bizarre individual stories are factually the truest parts. Overall, I am happy with the classification of these pages as 'faction'.

Early reviewers of first drafts of *Salad Days* suggested some parts of these reflections were nonsensical to non-cricket lovers. They required explanatory footnotes, or the bin. Though they are completely wrong, critics included my wife, who as ever requires indulgence and some thanks.

Another key bit of feedback I got was from a close friend, who commented on the draft, 'You do

know this will annoy a lot of people.'   I was very, very
proud.

Chapter 2 – The Torch of All Our Yesterdays

'The torch of all our yesterdays
Was kindled by a royal hand
To bear the Oriflamme always
And keep it splendid and ablaze
Was his command.'

Paisley Grammar School song – The Oriflamme

The midwife of these memoirs is Paisley Grammar School, locally known as 'the Grammar'. Paisley is the fifth most populous place in Scotland, with a world-famous 12th century abbey, its very own 'pattern', a fabulous range of historic buildings, and an international airport – often inaccurately labelled as 'Glasgow' airport. It is outrageously refused city status, despite this being awarded to small Scottish hamlets such as Stirling and Perth. Within Paisley, the Grammar School is a sort of 'institution' – and brings with it all positive and negative connotations of that term.

Founded by a Royal Chapter of James VI in 1576, it is certainly well established, and has evolved and grown continually since, in response to demand and advances in the Scottish education system. In recent times Paisley Grammar School was fee paying until the mid-1960s, just around the time I joined its now long defunct primary school. This fee-paying legacy was a problem in my time – with the changes clearly forced on a reluctant staff, who in so many ways tried to ignore and reverse the fact it was now becoming a dreaded 'comprehensive'.

It is a well recorded observation that the real snobs in society are not actually very rich people and aristocrats. It is the people who serve them and live off the system created. Bertie Wooster is not a snob, but Jeeves certainly is, and in country house dramas the snob supreme is commonly the butler. This is my roundabout way of introducing the 'servants' (aka teachers) of Paisley Grammar School in my time. The ways in which they sought to hold on to the trappings of fee-paying elitism were absurd. Fortunately it was like trying to hold back the tide, and I am sure this has now long gone.

But in the 1970s. the educational refuseniks were in full control. Letting in the 'lower orders' became unavoidable, but some rules and standards could still be enforced.

Top of the list was rugby. Paisley is a working-class town, famous for handloom weaving and with a proud history of radical politics. It is located in the football-mad heartlands of central Scotland. But the Grammar did not allow a football team in my time, with the extraordinary claim repeatedly made by senior staff that they could not sense any interest from pupils in this. I am fairly certain this was wrong, and though generally unimpressed with the intellect of most of the school's management, I am happy to classify this excuse as a straightforward 'lie' rather than outright stupidity. Here's a little bit of evidence: every break time, within seconds of the bell the playground was packed with as many impromptu games of football as it could fit in. I never once saw a rugby ball. What a strange and subtle way of demonstrating no interest in football.

Now, could this be that football was just a little 'working-class', unlike of course 'rugger'? Whilst technically no longer a public school, could we fool people by playing public school sports? This may seem to you a very weak strategy, but with all due respect, you probably never met the people in control of the Grammar school in the 1970s.

This is not to attack rugby – a sport I like to watch.[1] Rather it was the statement the school was making, and the assumption that if selected for the school's rugby team on a Saturday morning, this should automatically take precedence over anything else. Like, for example, playing for a non-school football team.

This had somewhat predictable consequences. One afternoon a week all boys in the school had to play a practice rugby match. This then determined selection for the school teams at the weekend. Rugby selection was viewed by the 'masters' as equivalent in standing to military conscription, and everyone knew this. Consequently, the key challenge in practice matches was to never have a good game.

It could become farcical. One day, I was passed a ball a yard from the try line, and without thinking, stupidly caught it. I could literally have fallen over for a try, and selection to play in a game I barely understood the rules of on a freezing Saturday morning beckoned. And nae fitba. What could I do, but turn round and run the other way. When questioned on this extraordinary reaction by the coach, I claimed an earlier, unnoticed head knock had

---

[1] At this point I can hear my wife shouting, 'And what fucken sport do you not like to watch?' I may have undermined my historic answer of 'Formula One' by repeatedly denouncing the idea that this is a sport. Clever engineering and computing no doubt, but a sport? Behave yourself – go and get it in the Olympics!

disorientated me. He said nothing at the time but picked me for the rugby team anyway. Bastard.

And of course, we played cricket – an uncommon sport in state schools in Scotland. This is just as well, as otherwise we would be without a book. It was greatly to my good fortune that I played this outwith the school and had developed some level of competence. It was also to my good fortune that many of my fellow pupils thought the idea of playing cricket was indicative of a low-level mental illness. Combined, these two facts meant it was relatively easy to get into the school cricket team.

This conferred advantages. It gave you a standing in the summer term with some of the delusional staff that saw cricket as a key bulwark against the inherent decline of the comprehensive system. Without doubt my disciplinary record appeared much better between March and June than in other terms, though my behaviour was unchanged. It also meant that time off studies in the spring and summer was plentiful.

Paisley Grammar had somehow maintained its playing status with Scotland's public sector school elite – for example, Hutchesons' Grammar in Glasgow, Morrison's Academy in Crieff, and pretty much all the schools in Edinburgh. To send a strong team to compete against these illustrious opponents was a key priority for the school – well beyond the importance of any teaching aspirations.

I was also lucky to be in a very strong generation for the school cricket team, and we won most of our matches – sometimes with embarrassing ease.

To many of the school's senior staff, a cricket winning streak of this type, against 'proper' schools, was truly orgasmic (or as near as they ever got to this state). It meant that when we set off on our coach to the most prestigious away games, the number of staff who had managed to swing the trip was extraordinary – teachers could outnumber players two to one. The opportunity to visit the promised land of public schools could not be resisted, and many I suspect doubled this up with an unsuccessful job interview. It was rumoured that on some of these afternoons, the shortage of staff remaining in the school meant janitors were press-ganged into taking Latin classes. Though unsubstantiated, it was reported that they conjugated verbs better, and were generally preferred to the absent teachers.

I enjoyed the privilege bestowed on me in school by playing cricket, though I suspect like most privilege quickly took it for granted. But it is only in much more recent years I have discovered another benefit this brought me. This was when I inadvertently met up with an old schoolmate in a pub after a St. Mirren game. After a ridiculously long time, we suddenly made the school connection, and Malky announced, 'I remember you now, you were one of these blue-blooded wankers that played cricket and got all the advantages. You used to pose about in your fancy barathea blazers with their tinsel. We are not worthy of your presence!' Now this may sound harsh, but it was all delivered and received in a spirit of inebriated comradeship, and as a way of introducing an interesting discussion theme.

My first response was perhaps a bit left field. 'What do you mean by tinsel?' 'Those fucken stripes you had on your jacket,' Malky replied. I had forgotten – school 'colours', and because I got into the first team quite young, I received an additional set every year. It was a nice memory, though I thought it best not to tell Malky, and I must say I did remember feeling quite dapper as the light blue colours set off my dark blue jacket.

But Malky had not yet got to the core of his bitterness. On our first reunion he had been accompanied by his grown-up daughter, which it turned out had edited his reflections. A few weeks later – without daughter – we were recovering in a pub after another emotionally draining experience watching St. Mirren. It was the whisky after the beer stage of the evening, and Malky returned to his theme:

'You married her – didn't you?'

'What?'

It all came out. Malky had been obsessed with my first wife who had been at school with us both. She had truly been his first 'crush'. But alas, I had triumphed in a competition neither me nor my wife had any idea actually existed.

'For months I waited, certain she'd tire of you, and I could make my move. But no, on you continued to prance about with your fancy blazer, and all your fancy-blazered pals. And of course, I noticed the wee smirks between you and her as the Rectum (see below) congratulated the cricket team at school assemblies on another win.'

He was not a happy man. My attempts to console him by suggesting other reasons why I had won the fair maiden – looks, wit, culture, and many more – were ruled out with utter disdain. The tinselled blazer alone had done it.

A few other things about the school's refusal to accept full comprehensive status further infuriated me. We did not have a 'headteacher' we had a 'Rector' – though in 1970s Scotland it did not take the greatest wit to change this to 'Rectum', and how much more appropriate that was. We did not have PE, we had 'field' – what the fuck is 'field'? Many of the classrooms were situated round a large oblong balcony area. But you could only walk one way around this - often meaning a journey of about a yard became a 100-yard sprint. When you got there, the very 'master' who had enforced this rule then upbraided you for running and being late. They liked their rules and power.

And in my primary school years I had to wear short trousers and a cap. In Paisley it might have been easier to simply attach a sign to my body: 'Fancy bullying a wee privileged twat? Here I am.'

Of the teaching, as often appeared in my reports, I now throwback to the refrain, 'Could do better.' I remember two outstanding teachers – one of maths (who sadly with me was always fighting a losing battle), and one of history (who wasn't). The rest of the teaching was simply uninspiring. This partly lay I think with an approach which aimed to maximise exam results rather than learning, and at this time the Grammar probably did OK in this regard.

Where I cannot accept this excuse was in the teaching of English – particularly English literature. I can only assume that at one point a staff circular was issued that the core objective of the English Department was to make sure no pupil ever read a novel voluntarily again. Parrot class reading of random sections of Carson McCullers' *The Member of the Wedding* was simply not going to cut it with a group of Paisley 14-year-olds. The idea that a largely disinterested teacher thought it would be, is beyond comprehension. To his credit, however, he was very keen on rugby and field.

But without the intervention of an unlikely heroine, all my reflections on Paisley Grammar School may have been in the past tense. In 1987, in response to falling school numbers, Strathclyde Regional Council suggested closing the school. A lot of people were not happy, and the school had a number of influential pals and former pupils who formed a vigorous 'save the school' campaign. Step forward someone without a strong fan base in the town: UK premier Margaret Thatcher. She insisted on a change to legislation which kept my alma mater open.

Personally, I was ambiguous about school closure. For me the Grammar had no given right to survive, and I have noted above some concerns on certain aspects of its operation. But in the end, it was 'my school'. This ultimately led me to decline an offer to become a political activist in a counter campaign *for* school closure planned by a close friend: 'Shut it – it's Shite!' I politely turned down an office bearing role in his nascent movement, though respectfully praising the directness of the campaign slogan. I do not think he has ever forgiven me for my betrayal, though his formal response that I had become a 'running dog of capitalism' seemed a bit extreme. This led me to call out his personal betrayal of trust in another refrain of the school song, which was deliberately sourced to dial up his anger:

> *'The torch has ever burned with light*
> *Inspiring, down the days of dust.*
> *They held it sacred in his sight.*
> *To pass it on, a beacon bright:*
> *It was their trust.'*

Paisley Grammar School has some famous former pupils, which is hardly surprising given how long it's been around. Clearly the OGs in these memoirs are the most famous, alongside my long-term secret adversary Malky. But some reasonable contenders are in the runner-up slots, including one giant.

Without exaggeration, I can fairly claim our wee school significantly contributed to the collapse of the world financial order in 2008; pioneered space and time travel; failed – through no fault of its own – to reverse the catastrophic outcome of the 2019 UK General Election; and changed for all time the political dynamic of Scotland's capital city.

'How so?' I hear you cry. I will justify these claims in order.

OG and former knight of the realm Fred Goodwin was the lavish spending CEO of the Royal Bank of Scotland Group. In the early 2000s he achieved celebrity status by overseeing a massive expansion of the bank through an aggressive acquisition strategy. Sadly, despite Fred's accountancy background, it did not end well: the numbers did not quite seem to add up. In early 2008, the banking group announce a staggering loss of £24.1 billion, contributing to a world financial meltdown and the worst recession since the Second World War.

Journalist Nick Cohen summed up that Fred had gone out of fashion by noting that '…he left the UK taxpayer with unlimited liability for the cost of clearing up the mess.' On the one hand, there are clearly some problems with Fred's legacy; but on the other, he did without question make a big impact.

OG David Tennant is an outstanding and multi-talented actor. He is perhaps most famous as the tenth Doctor Who (for many the best) – taking further the world's progress in time travel and all things unknown, and generally seeing off some pretty bad things. David's commitment to the Doctor should not be underestimated; he is married to the daughter of the fifth Doctor, Peter Davison.

I have a very tenuous personal connection to David. My first wife and I were married by his father Sandy McDonald, a very charismatic preacher, and once Moderator of the General Assembly of the Church of Scotland. How often have I dined out on the line, 'I was married by Doctor Who's dad!' Some close friends have cruelly suggested it is my sole claim to fame.

OG Andrew Neil is a renowned journalist and broadcaster, and son of a former millworker in Paisley. Though a tad to the right for my liking, it would be churlish not to recognise that as a political interviewer he is amongst the best in the business. His reputation is based on rigorous research, and a persistent and forensic line of enquiry that has often left even the most adept politicians in pieces.

So given his reputation, it is far from surprising that a less than adept politician such as Boris Johnson would be 'bricking it' in considering an important 1:1 election interview. But sadly, chief advisor and travel writer Dominic Cummings – realising he could not be present to wipe his arse during the inevitable road crash – came up with the fabulous idea of just not showing up. Incredibly it worked, despite the BBC's feisty comeback that they were 'a bit disappointed.' What might have been if Andrew had got to the brave, fearless, patriotic clown who then (in theory) ran the country.

OG Alex Wood is likely to be lesser known to readers, but his political contribution is significant. Flicking through the pages of the school's annual *Grammarian* magazine, a glance at the 'News of former pupils' would find little reference to this diminutive Dundonian. For a period (which strangely seemed to end about 2008), this really became the 'Fred Goodwin appreciation page', and historically, other plaudits were awarded to former pupils achieving such mighty deeds as removing teeth, counting well in offices, and selling lots of potatoes. So why no mention in 1984 of wee Alex becoming leader of the City of Edinburgh District Council? The answer is easy: he was a disgrace. He was the first ever Labour leader in our capital city, and to boot, a former member of the Militant Tendency.

It was touch and go for a period, but the Grammar survived. As did Labour in Edinburgh; the Tories have never controlled the city since, though in recent years the SNP have contributed to maintaining this impressive record.

I happened to be a junior officer in Edinburgh City Council during Alex's political leadership. It was fun, and at a time when Edinburgh was at the forefront of Council opposition to Thatcher's budget cuts by potentially setting illegal rates. It was a politically charged and high-profile atmosphere. Prior to 1984, it was just assumed the Tories would run Edinburgh, and over many years a group of senior Council officers had been established who did their bidding in a quiet uncontroversial way – ensuring through studied inaction that wealth and privilege remained as God intended with the chosen few.

Actually, they were a nice, friendly group of old men (of course) – patrician in standing, and well dressed in a sort of Downton Abbey vibe. Alex and his colleagues' arrival was like a bombshell that they never initially noticed, and from which they never subsequently recovered. At the first meeting they shuffled in to be faced by a group of very politically motivated, and to them exceptionally young, people. Even worse, some of them were women, and they were clutching this strange new thing – a 'manifesto' with policies and actions they wanted their officers to implement.

But my favourite memory of Alex is a less overtly political story, and a general lesson in negotiating skills. Before any difficult discussions, business strategy textbooks suggest you take control of the *tone* of a meeting and try and wrong foot potential adversaries. Alex had just flown back from a crisis meeting of the Labour Party Executive in London, and by way of an ice breaker, the Council Chief Executive asked if he'd had a good journey. Alex mentioned that he was not an experienced flyer, and then added, 'Have you ever had a shite on a plane? It's a really weird experience.' Alex had taken control of the meeting, and the city.

Alex, and all the former pupils mentioned, have much to commend them, but there can only be one stand out. This was unknown to me before beginning my research, and in itself was worth all the effort. It demands its own paragraph.

The late and great Kenny Ireland was an OG!

This is perhaps not an immediately familiar name but is in fact the actor who played the legendary Donald Stewart in the classic and massively underrated TV sitcom *Benidorm*.[2] Now, whilst

Tennant is without question an outstanding actor, can anyone really suggest he can match the superbly charming, loveable, overweight, opportunistic, swinger that Ireland created in 'Donald'? I think not. How proud I am that Donald was an OG in the wider sense, and how well he would have fitted into the collection of eccentric entertainers honoured later in these chronicles.

---

[2] It is perhaps a sad reflection on my declining years that I once came close to starting a pub brawl through my dogmatic insistence that *Benidorm* is amongst the finest pieces of television ever crafted. Things came to a head when I dismissively labelled those suggesting it was just a modern *Carry On* film as intellectually incapable of appreciating *Benidorm*'s many layers and messages for modern times. If you have not watched, do so – all nine series. And then decide which side you would have been on if the punches had started flying. Sadly, Kenny died after series 6, and with him the legend that was Donald Stewart. Kenny was also in the classic Victoria Wood sketch *Acorn Antiques*.

Chapter 3 – Building a team

'I will not cease from Mental Fight,
Nor shall my Sword sleep in my hand;
'Till we have built Jerusalem.'

William Blake/Frank Uber (OG AGM, February 1977)

In any team sport a pretty non-negotiable requirement and starting point is a team. In cricket this involves mustering 11 players every game.

For many people not involved in club cricket it is difficult to imagine just how hard this can be - especially if you are ploughing the pretty thin soil of Scotland. This is connected to the fact that too many people are just fat and lazy. In a club cricket context this is doubly frustrating, without giving it a go many people never discover it is possible to be fat and lazy and still play.

Recruitment was a never-ending struggle for the Old Grammarians Cricket Club – globally branded as the OGs. It inevitably led to wide and indiscriminate player targeting with few, if any, criteria.

This was intensified beyond press-ganging levels when the 1977 AGM came to the radical, if somewhat counterintuitive conclusion, that the numerical (and general) weakness of the first XI was because we didn't have a 'feeder' second XI. The motion was of course proposed by club legend and local undertaker Frank Uber. Frank was the guy many amateur sport teams need. He was a hopeless cricketer - only ever drafted in for the most severe emergencies. But what he lacked in playing ability he more than made up for in a massive love of the game, endless energy, and relentless persistence. Without Frank none of these memoirs would have been written, because there would have been no OGs.

Frank introduced his proposal.

'What we need is a flow of talent cutting their teeth at a lower level; not quite ready for the white-hot heat of top team action, but learning, and putting some pressure on the guys in the firsts. I've noticed some complacency recently; maybe feeling competition from up-and-coming young bucks might be what some regulars need.'

'You mean young people...like under 30?' Alf Gibbs was perhaps one player aware of this potential pressure. Controversially holding on to the pivotal number 3 slot (commonly the team's best player), his batting average of 5.66 in the previous season[3] was leading to increased dressing room whispers that he may be more effective down the order against an older ball.[4]

'Unlikely, I think,' chimed in Dougie Caper after Frank's initial input.

Dougie, who followed Alf at four in the increasingly vulnerable engine shed[5] of the batting line up, could always be counted on to back his old pal. They came from the same generation of OGs, and their bond had been strengthened further by a recent move to the same care home.

But the motion was passed. Frank's relentless enthusiasm and optimism normally carried the day. His record and reputation for player recruitment was legendary. Few people between the ages of 11 and 87 were exempt. He was unconscious of any bias for

---

[3] Not good, you would want this figure to be over 30.
[4] Batting is generally anticipated to get easier later in an innings as the ball softens. But this comment is actually another way of confirming Alf was by this stage a very poor player.
[5] The players who bat at 3 and 4 are often the best batsman. This was obviously not the case with Alf and Dougie.

any reason – age, ethnicity, sexuality, gender, or disabilities. All were welcomed - or more accurately potential victims. In his unconscious way, he was an equal opportunities visionary.

In the fevered recruitment days following creation of the second XI, all criteria were abandoned. First to go was, 'Do you, or have you ever, played cricket?' In the west of Scotland this was often a pretty fundamental deal breaker. A second softer replacement question then fronted approaches: 'Do you know what cricket is?' This was slightly more effective. But it generated some negative feedback, not uncommonly accompanied by very unfortunate 1980s terminology on the inquirer's sexuality.

These two approaches appeared to secure three new recruits. But one subsequently said he was so drunk he had no recollection of the conversation, whilst a second had taken a more positive spin on the sexuality issue and thought Frank had indirectly been asking him out. The third was a genuine recruit, Robin Credit, a local carpet salesman. But, by late April Robin was unavailable for the next three years due, he claimed, to 'a corrupt defence lawyer'.

So, the final recruitment card was played: a clever double headed question. Initially: 'Do you have any friends?' Secondly: 'If not, would you like 10 guys to kid on they are your friends on Saturday afternoons in the summer?' This approach was more effective. It led, for example, to the recruitment of Gavin Bland, whom we return to in a later chapter.

Based on these very loose criteria, the individual stories of Frank Uber's recruitment endeavours were extraordinary - and some may also be true.

Bundling young guys into his camper van – in full cricket kit at the end of their morning school game – was commonplace. Lest there be any misunderstandings here, and accusations beyond the minor crime of abduction, the camper van also normally contained Frank's wife, his two young children, and a number of dogs.

It is in this context that his offer to the bemused schoolboys of 'a day at the seaside and an ice cream' needs to be interpreted: the OGs were three men short for an afternoon away game at the coastal town of Prestwick. It is also in this context that we can best understand Frank's tempting offer that one of the boys 'could be batting as high as nine.'[6]

---

[6] With only 8 other players, this is quite likely.

A potentially more worrying recruitment episode involved a Glasgow Corporation bus.

As people familiar with the obscure and minority west of Scotland pastime known as 'cricket' will know, many of the finest players in the world are from Asian backgrounds, where it is not such an obscure and minority activity. The great Indian batsman Sachin Tendulkar has a level of fame a Beatle would have craved. He is known by many as 'Little God'. They are not wrong – in fact I don't think 'Big God' would have taken strike.[7]

Thanks to Sachin - and quite a few others – any Asian guy became very vulnerable to Frank's recruitment strategy. I guess you could categorise this as 'positive discrimination', but to Frank it was simply based on a theory that it improved his chances of snaring another player – who may be very good.

In this he was not always wrong; over the years, the OGs benefitted from many fine Asian players. Two stalwarts owned a curry house in Paisley, a piece of information I suspect they then regretted sharing. The consequences of this are returned to later in these chronicles.

---

[7] Normally the better opening batsman takes 'strike'. Sachin really was that good.

Frank's approach to Asian recruitment was possibly simplistic, but generally well-meaning and not entirely ineffective. But in his enthusiasm, he could overstep the line.

One spring day, Frank boarded a Glasgow Corporation bus on the outskirts of the city, driven by a young Sikh who we subsequently discovered was called Yuvraj. This immediate recruitment trigger was then nuclearised when he noticed the newspaper next to the driver was open at the cricket pages.

It is a pity the threatened court case was not progressed, as this account would be more accurate. What appeared to have happened was something like this.

'Ah, I see you are interested in cricket,' Frank said as he boarded the bus.

'Yes, very much, but it's not much of a thing in Glasgow. I do kind of miss it,' replied Yuvraj, making his first mistake.

Frank was beginning to slightly overheat. 'Oh no, much more cricket here than you'd think. Do you play?'

Yuvraj was trying to drive a bus. 'I did, but look sir, I don't want to be rude, but you can't really stand there when the bus is moving. It's not allowed. It's quiet now, but it will fill up as we get into town.'

'Of course, but while it's quiet, what are you - a batter or bowler?' persisted Frank.

'Well, a bit of both actually. But please, you need to move.' Yuvraj had made his second and fatal error.

Frank was now visibly sweating. 'Of course, but if I could just give you this number. Saturdays, Sundays, a few weeknights, and we could get you a lift if needed.'

'I can't see, take that out of my sight!'

It was only a small bump as the bus hit the side of the shelter, and fortunately no-one was hurt. Damage ran to a few hundred pounds. Frank took the full blame and paid up, and Yuvraj was happy to leave it there. That appeared to be the end of it.

Two years later, however, before a big cup game, an ashen-faced Frank appeared in our dressing room after welcoming the opponents and said, 'He's here! Remember the Indian bus driver Yuvraj that bats and bowls a bit? He's opening the bowling and is rumoured to be quick and hostile. He recognised me and gave me a menacing smile.'

We lost the toss and were put into bat. 35 minutes later, our cup run was over. Yuvraj could indeed 'bowl a bit' and seemed surprisingly motivated. We did not manage to test if he could bat.[8]

But undeterred, Frank's relentless and endless recruitment drive continued.

It is a great, and often underrated, achievement how many amateur sports teams manage to regularly field the requisite number of players, irrespective of the context. And no context, at face value, was less promising than asking people to commit up to eight hours on a summer Saturday and Sunday to play for a low-level Scottish cricket team. But I can think of very few occasions when we didn't have the necessary eleven in some form.

So how did this work? Having someone like Frank Uber on board was certainly critical, but this had to coincide with an understanding of what individual motivations and reasons led a vastly diverse

---

[8] If you have scored very few runs as a team batting first, commonly not many of the other team require to bat to ensure you have been soundly humped.

crew of creatures to turn out for the OGs over the years.   Answering this has perhaps required the hardest thinking in any part of these chronicles. After long reflection, I suggest the following list. For many OGs, more than one of these motivations came together – 'synergy' I believe is the word.

Attending Paisley Grammar School

Over the years, the school was the main source of personnel, although never by itself supplying enough people to make a team. Whilst in the context of the OGs these things are relative, this source normally produced the most sensible core of players, people who had played a bit of cricket at school and wished to continue playing in their adult years. As an OG, why not play for the OGs – unless you were very good? This group were known as the 'blue bloods'; they provided some level of stability (boredom) around which the many eccentrics could work their magic.

Random geography

Although qualifying in category one, this is where I would most position my journey to the OGs. As mentioned in the opening chapter, I was born next to a cricket field and played from my earliest memories. It was just the natural thing to do.

But I am a minority element of the 'random geography' category; the majority of players sourced in this way were people from other 'proper' cricket playing countries who happened to pitch up in the Paisley area. This was the second most fertile seam of OG recruits, consisting of some normal and often good cricketers, but also contributing solidly to our cadre of eccentrics.

In terms of geographic origin, the most numerous source of players was England, closely followed by those whose families came from the Asian sub-continent. Less frequently, we also had players from the West Indies, South Africa, Ireland, Wales and – as we return to below – a very brief input from a solitary Bermudian. Perhaps surprisingly, we did not have any Australians. One theory expounded for this was that they were all tied to their TV screens watching endless reruns of the outrageously racist UK TV sitcom *Love Thy Neighbour*.

A significant cohort of the English category were academics at Glasgow's outstanding universities. Inevitably this skyrocketed our official eccentricity rating. In my memory, none were ever remotely young, and many were amongst the worst cricketers imaginable. In compensation, some were clearly very well quoted in their field – including departmental heads and senior professors. When you could understand what they were saying, it was often very funny. Looking back, I have a theory, on which I think one of the up-and-coming new breed of academics could perhaps hone their critical analysis skills. In summary, the thesis question is: 'The better the academic, the worse the cricketer?' If someone ever picks up the baton here, please include me as a consultee.

Personal unpleasantness

This was a less common, but nonetheless significant source of OG recruits.

In cricket you spend a lot of time with your teammates in the summer months: it is a very long game and can involve quite a bit of travelling time. In Scotland, it also involves endless hours sitting in a bleak dressing room watching the rain or snow, and with little else to do. Now, in these circumstances, who do you want in your trench? Answer I suspect for most – someone entertaining and likeable.

If you are the opposite of this, after a while your colleagues may begin to suggest – with greater or lesser degrees of subtlety – that you may wish to look for another club. At its most extreme, this in Scotland is reduced to the very blunt phrase that it was time for the offender to 'do one'.[9] Consequently, through these dynamic human interactions, some players were released into the market for other more desperate clubs.

Shrewd recruiters – with none shrewder than Frank Uber – were on to the early warning signs of someone likely to be 'doing one'. Frank would commonly tutor senior players on how to track personal discord in opposing teams during games – and if any single player was the repeated cause of this. It was often quite easy. For example:

(1) On-field physical assault – uncommon but not impossible – between opposing players. A dropped, easy catch could trigger this – especially if was the fifth such failure of the game.

(2) Reaction to a run out suggesting that this is a repeat offence, accompanied by a shouted line from the departing batsman such as, 'That's the fucken last time that bastard will ever do that to me!' Frank awarded bonus points to anyone alert enough to report that this outburst was from the opposing team's captain.

(3) Someone being repeatedly placed in a fielding position on the boundary and as far away as

---

[9] Alternative terminology here includes the offender being told to 'get tae!'

possible from any colleagues for the full three hours of the innings, irrespective of how far this requires running between overs.[10] A variation of this was the exact opposite – repeatedly forcing someone to field very close to a good batsman against a very poor bowler. This almost certainly guaranteed personal injury as the batsmen hit an easy ball very hard at very vulnerable parts of your anatomy.

(4) Not very subtle off field hints of unpopularity. For example, after the game the offensive player popping his head round your dressing room door and saying, 'Bit of a mix up...by the time I came out the shower, all my guys have headed-off and seem to have forgotten about me. Any of you folks going near the southside of Glasgow?'

At one level, you may think that through this we may have recruited some quite good players – someone good at cricket but weak on other essential life skills. Alas this was not the case; many teams would tolerate a complete arse with cricketing ability, but hunt someone without this or personal decency.

---

[10] A bit of logic. At the end of each over a cricket match reverses, and the ball is bowled from the opposite end of the wicket. In effect everything is turned around. So if you are fielding in one position far behind the batsmen, to field in the same position in the next over you must run the entire length of the field. This can require a jog of about 120 yards every three minutes. Would anyone that liked you expect you to do that?

Only when these attributes were both absent, did we have our man.

Why, you may ask, would the OGs want someone with these characteristics? The first reason was simply how desperate we often were. The second is much more positive: in the jovial, witty and humane company of his new OG peers, all such recruits would quickly become thoroughly decent chaps. I don't think that we ever improved anyone's cricketing ability: but this is of minor consequence.

Fitness

This motivation is double edged, and not as it may first appear. Scotland has a particular strength in ensuring many men of a certain age grow outward. Vague and erroneous references to thyroid issues seldom convince, and the brutal truths of overeating, alcohol consumption, and a sedentary lifestyle become unavoidable. The criticisms of family and friends – so often disguised as 'motivation' – lead to suggestions of taking up something more active. Thoughts of running, five-a-side football, tennis, swimming, and hill climbing induce cold sweats; whilst current activities such as darts, snooker, and dominoes are derided as serious 'sporting' options.

And then one summer's day you accidently happen upon a club cricket game. As a Scot, it is likely that you have very little idea of what is going on, and initially think, 'What the fuck is that?' But it looks curiously quaint, and your customary three lunchtime pints have given you a sense of bonhomie. You watch on. Recalibrating your initially dismissive reaction, you then accept that in a sort of 'nothing is really happening' way, these guys seem to be enjoying themselves. And suddenly a eureka thought blasts into your consciousness: 'Look at the size of some of these fuckers!'

'Great sport, cricket,' you announce to your completely uninterested partner. 'Suppose so,' she replies. Result – she has accepted it is a 'sport'.

Fortunately, you have arrived at the end of an innings, and the teams stroll off. Though you are unaware at the time, they are heading for the ritual of 'tea' – to gorge themselves on sandwiches, cakes, and crisps.[11] Skipping round the boundary and feeling sort of trim for the first time in years, you catch up with one of the players.

'Can you tell me who's in charge here?' you ask.

---

[11] The title of this book, *Salad Days*, has nothing to do with cricket teas. Any misunderstanding here could not be more wrong.

'Barry, I suppose, our captain. Barry, someone wanting you.'

Over waddles Barry, and you quickly think, 'Oh, maybe there is a rule that the biggest of all needs to be captain?'

'Hi,' he says. 'Barry Wardrop, but I'm better known as Lard. How can I help?'

'I was interested in whether there was any chance you sometimes needed players. Is there an audition or something?'

Barry beams. 'What are you doing next Saturday?'

'Well, nothing, but to be honest I've never really played cricket. Not that sure of the rules even.'

Barry stretches out his hand. 'See you Saturday. 1pm.'

Barry turns and scurries off to the buffet. You have your sport, and the answer to your critics. And in this way, the OGs have gathered another recruit.

This fitness issue is predominantly, but perhaps not exclusively, a feature of amateur club cricket.

A few years ago, I was watching the Cricket
World Cup finals on TV. It was a group game between
Bermuda and Australia. It was of limited interest as
Australia would always be too strong for Bermuda,
and the outcome was inevitable. Nevertheless, this
was the World Cup, and to any cricketers at my level,
everyone on show was comparatively an exceptional
player. It was just that in this company Bermuda
were 'minnows'.

But I looked again and realised that in another
context, labelling Bermuda's cricketers as 'minnows'
could not be more wrong. This was a group with
some seriously chunky chaps; in some the cases the
'fat' word came to mind. From a starting position of
some disinterest, I began to root for the Bermudians
with great intent. They were actually doing quite
well, and – building on years of delusion from
following the Scottish national football side – I began
to think the impossible was in sight. Sadly, the world
intervened, and Bermuda lost by some margin. But I
became a fan for life.

Now this, by chance, is consistent with the
only Bermudian to have 'played' for the OGs. It was a
very brief career, and I cannot recall how he came to
the club, or his full name. I think his first name was

David. I do remember, however, why his stay was so brief.

There was some excitement at his recruitment; Bermuda did after all play cricket. As he emerged for his debut from teammate Denzil's new MG, it became apparent he was in the 'very big unit' category that I now know to be characteristic of many cricketers from that sub-tropical paradise.

It was a short evening game which we won comfortably. David neither batted or bowled and fielded at slip – the most sedentary position available. I am fairly sure he never touched the ball, and yet he was never selected for the OGs again. Why? On the Monday after the game, Denzil sent the club a formal request for financial assistance to replace the suspension on the passenger side of his new car. This was refused, and so were any alternative approaches to teammates to transport David to future games. Given his bulk, public transport options were problematical. Our only Bermudian was an OG no more[12].

---

[12] I once mentioned these reflections to a work colleague who had lived and had family in Bermuda. Humorous, I thought. She passed these on to her Bermudian brother-in-law, who immediately replied that if I ever set foot on the island he would personally kill me. I think he was called David.

Marital discord/complications

This factor could both strengthen and weaken our team. It is also surprisingly multi-dimensional. As we have established, cricket is a long game, with the added complication you are never entirely sure how long it will last. You can play an awful lot of games in mid-summer. With travelling included, two weekend and two weeknights could account for a total of approaching 25 hours a week. Assuming an average of eight hours sleep a night, cricket at its peak could take up over 22% of your waking hours.[13]

Clearly this can impact on anyone who is in a serious relationship.

The least interesting aspect of this is the inconvenience of happy and balanced relationships and marriages.

These relationships can *compete* for time with cricket.[14] This is arguably not unreasonable. In the 1980s and 1990s we were probably still in a more traditional 'dating' mode. At a certain age, a relationship would emerge that may be 'the one'. But this was often surrounded by doubt and insecurity on

---

[13] I am indebted to former OG Professor Adrian Summs for help in these calculations.

[14] You may argue only a cricketer could ask this question this way round.

both sides. In this context, the ardent cricketer suitor was required to craft a tricky statement; something like:

'Now you know I really love you and want to spend my life with you. But between late April and early September, I may not be around much every Saturday and Sunday, and one or two nights a week. And even on weekend evenings we can't really organise anything, as I'm never sure when the cricket will finish. I know it's the key, romantic summer months, but think Indian summers, and that lovely early spring we had this year.'

It may not go down too well. In this event, and I speak from experience, the following softening line is probably best avoided: 'That said, if you're desperate to see me you could always come and help with the teas.'

And then children could come along. Frank Uber automatically logged any births, to ensure an alert was triggered for the date when, in an emergency, anyone over eight could be drafted into an away friendly. But there were interim and longer-term selection problems with OGs breeding. Hard as it was for some of the older members – educated whilst the school was still fee paying – they bowed to the inevitable, and finally accepted that fathers were expected to make some sort of contribution to child rearing.

Occasionally fatherhood ended cricketing careers, but often some compromise was reached. This did not include, however, approval at an AGM of a controversial motion that all OGs should focus future procreation activities to maximise childbirths in the most parentally demanding winter months. As a sign of more liberal days ahead, this was soundly defeated.

Less stable relationships tend to be preferable for cricket team selectors. This includes the category of the player who sees playing cricket as many blessed hours of escape from a relationship that is not working. He is available for all games, making him popular with selectors.

In my experience these are commonly sad downtrodden folk, consistently bemoaning their partner for pathetically minor reasons. It can become their USP. In the OGs, this was overwhelmingly to do with heterosexual relationships, and the offending partner very seldom got beyond being 'she' or 'her'.

This, frankly, annoyed me. I was often close to bursting out, 'Well you fucking married her!' or, 'If it's that bad, get out of it!' At some point you would then meet the offending spouse, and two things were quite apparent. Firstly, in a good way they were nothing like the person portrayed; and secondly, your teammate was terrified and overawed by them. Words such as 'pet', 'dear', 'princess', 'darling' were excruciatingly overused in a clawingly, ingratiating way – never a good sign in a relationship.

What was going on in these relationships on a wider level also helped OG selections. As the saying goes, 'It takes two to tango', or not. In the 1980s, it would seldom have occurred to my teammates just why a 'dreadful' partner was so happy for them to play cricket all the time – freeing up *their* Saturdays, Sundays, and weeknights. This was of course because the wrongly criticised spouse was even more happy to have all this time to themselves.

A short-lived teammate called Maurice Grimm, recruited via the 'personal unpleasantness' route, brought the reality of this home to a wider audience. As he bored us senseless one day during a rain break about how awful his wife was, a teammate trying to be more positive commented, 'Well at least she's very reasonable in letting you play all this cricket. Kind of surprising really.' There followed one of the best silences I can remember, as we all looked at Maurice and realised Mrs Grimm's behaviour was not surprising at all.

Spouses allowing OGs to play lots of cricket was most commonly motivated by the innocent 'bored out my napper with him' scenario. But the combination of tiring relationships and lots of spare time on your own can also result in darker developments. Once these came very close to home for the OGs and impacted directly on a key season.

Lesley and Joe Bright were both former pupils at the Grammar. They married aged 20, after an 11-year school-based relationship. In retrospect, it should have been more obvious that they were not suited. Lesley was a loud, gregarious, party-going redhead, making her way in nursing. Joe was a decent, quiet, biochemist, heavily involved in stamp collecting and his local church. Joe drank very little; Lesley made up the shortfall.

Joe had come through the OG cricketing ranks from school - a dependable left arm bowler. Although he considered himself fast medium, in truth his wickets mainly came from being much slower than he initially appeared.

Into their already fading relationship entered a newer OG recruit, Benny Gladstone, a rake thin, tall, and flamboyant Kilmacolm greengrocer. With hooded eyes, chalk white colouring, and jet black hair, he had a nose that could have invented the word 'beak'.

Once again a nickname came easily: 'Vampire'. As a cricketer he was an unreliable, attacking batsmen, not known for long innings but sometimes making some useful contributions.

The love triangle that became 'Bright-Gladstonegate' was uncovered in a strange way. An impromptu pub selection meeting was in trouble; it was convened in the middle of the peak summer holiday period, and options were very limited. On any calculation, both Joe and Benny had to play to get us up to 11 men.

'To be honest, I can't ever remember Joe and Benny playing in the same team,' I innocently observed.

'No,' piped up colleague Denzil, 'and you'd think being brothers-in-law they'd be keen to play together.' Denzil was not the sharpest OG, as will be demonstrated in some detail later.

There was a pause before two or three of us simultaneously blurted out: 'Brothers-in-law?'

All eyes turned to Denzil.

'Yes, I accidently ran into Benny and Lesley in an Italian restaurant in Edinburgh earlier in the year.

It was dark, but I recognised them and went over. They were sitting close, and just until I approached appeared to be holding hands. I said hello. In a higher pitched voice than normal, Benny replied hurriedly that he was making sure his sister was having a good birthday.'

How lucky they were at the time that it was only Denzil. But now this information had reached wider and much more dangerous ears. Not only had this sibling relationship between Benny and Lesley never been mentioned, when Lesley appeared at games or at social nights she gave the impression that she barely knew Benny. We did not need to check if Poirot was still alive to solve the puzzle, nor to be assisted by OG Tron's evidence that Lesley had once expressed an interest in Hammer House of Horrors films.

'Aha!' pronounced club thinker Trevor Stone, stroking a beard he did not actually have. 'Not good for getting a team this weekend, but perhaps very, very useful longer-term information. I will have a word with Frank Uber.'

Keeping this information secret had no selection value to the OGs. Telling Joe would probably have resulted in neither he nor Benny playing again. Telling Benny may have meant, on the grounds of chivalry, he may leave. Only one person could help the OGs' cause – Lesley.

I suspect it was a difficult phone call – but Frank was an undertaker, so in a sense on home ground. It was very simple: Lesley's dalliance with Benny had been outed. But the OGs were nothing if not reasonable; we were not going to tell Joe, and we were not even going to suggest she ended the affair. No, our only condition was solely cricket related. Joe and Benny were very different cricketers - one strengthened the bowling, and one the batting. Which of these was more valuable varied from game to game, depending on the availability of other players. Lesley was invited on to the selection committee, and asked to commit to arranging her subsequent activities around the team's week-by-week needs.

She was given 24 hours to make a decision. With a gun against her head, feisty Lesley came out fighting, initially claiming she was going to come clean and set up a regular threesome. 'The OGs would be well fucked then,' she commented, as I supposed would she. But eventually, she backed down and played along.

Lesley had the last laugh. Early in the following season she started a further affair with our best all round player. She didn't even like him.

Deception

This was amongst the less frequent factors in OG recruitment. It stemmed from some of our darkest moments when we just had to accept we couldn't find anyone else interested in cricket. Answer – get them along for other reasons, and just sort of slip the cricket in. This wasn't easy.

It succeeded to a degree through asking someone to come for a drink, and then indicating you'd forgotten to mention that this was linked to a cricket game. But as the tale of Bob Blackstock recalls later, it meant that even if successful, the recruit was so drunk by the start of the game it was self-defeating.

Other pathetically unsuccessful attempts in this category included claiming that whilst fielding in certain positions you could see naked swinger parties in a nearby garden. Though I have no doubt these were plentiful in prosperous 1980s Kilmacolm, garden gates were high and very well secured.

A final deception tried without success was to claim a very famous person was turning out for the opposition. For example, we once suggested ex-Beatle George Harrison was a likely starter for a Merseyside touring team; and on another occasion that Archbishop Desmond Tutu had stayed on after a speaking engagement in Glasgow and was guesting for visiting side Clydesdale. On reflection we aimed too high; if we'd limited it to, say, a Krankie or a Bay City Roller, it may have worked.

Blackmail

Low indeed, and not favoured by other than by the most unscrupulous selectors. Thankfully it was an infrequently used mechanism.

Comrade Henry Sherwood was perhaps the most unfair victim of this heinous tactic. His story is told in full later. Besotted by the mature, irresistible, revolutionary communist Natasha, he always felt his relationship hinged on a 100% devotion to the cause – in thought, word, and deed. But his Achilles heel was an addiction to the racing pages of a Rupert Murdoch-owned daily paper. This habit was happily fed to him by his OG teammates, and he would quietly sit secretly in a dressing room corner with the paper selecting his cuddies. 'Natasha need never know,' we assured him with oily smiles.

Not, of course, until we had the unenviable task of finding 11 lunatics to turn out for our traditional season-opening fixture at Kirkcaldy, on the east coast of Scotland. Their ground is placed high above the town. On balmy summer days I am sure it has lovely views out over the North Sea. We were never asked on balmy summer days, but as pre-season fodder in the third week of April. The North Sea was seldom visible.

Frank Uber, as ever, summed up the dishonesty inherent in getting a team. As the fixture card appeared for yet another season, there it was again – confirming T.S. Eliot's musing on April being the 'cruellest month':

Sunday, 19/4 – Kirkcaldy (away) (friendly).

'Come on, Frank, no-one wants to play that one. It's miles away and bloody freezing. And we always get hammered.'

'Not at all, boys, it's a tradition we always keep up. And my memory is that we very often get a lovely, freak early summer's day for it.'

By the time of the fixture, however, Frank's position had subtly changed, as he phoned round designated drivers to consider going up and staying over on the Saturday night in case the roads were blocked by snow ploughs.

And every year we went, shivered miserably, caught cold, and got humped. There was only ever one upside: as the weaker side, we always bowled first in the period up to tea about 5pm. For most of this time this was only in a slightly increasing sleet. By the time we came to bat from about 5.30pm - when at any point nine of us were in the comparative warmth of the dressing room - it was more blanket snow. Small mercies.

So back to the power of blackmail. 'Team for Sunday at Kirkcaldy,' selector Tron announced at the pre-season get together. 'I can't seem to find any blank paper, so I'll just use this old newspaper. 'Number one.' Tron licked his bookie's pencil and raised *The Sun* racing pages in the air. 'You OK, Henry Sherwood?' It worked every time.

Witness protection

By definition, it is clearly quite tricky to put a number on the OGs who joined us as part of the Witness Protection Scheme.

In principle it's not a bad idea. Presumably people on these schemes need some sort of life, but a low profile, and one that does not draw too much attention to them. Getting outside must be good – especially in the summer. And something that in Scotland few people take any notice of must be handy. Just writing this, I am convinced playing cricket for an obscure team like the OGs is in fact a genius witness protection option – it meets pretty much every requirement. As I reflect further, I wonder just how many of the guys I played with could have been on this. It would explain a great deal.

But for sure,[15] I know of only one. The perhaps obviously named John Brown. The evidence falls into four parts.

Firstly, he said as few words as it is possible for any human being to utter – monosyllabic doesn't quite do it. Some examples of questions and responses were:

How are you doing? – OK.

Have you ever played cricket before? – Yes.

Are you a batter or a bowler? – Batter.
What do you do for a living? – Work.

Where do you live? – Around here.

What is your wife's name? – Mrs Brown.

I am going to the buffet; do you want me to get you anything? – Food.

Do you want a lift home? – No.

Do you want to go for a pint? – No.

That was pretty much it. The longest sentence I ever heard him say was when I was batting with him. He clipped a nice shot off his legs and shouted, 'Two runs, wait, no, just one.' It was a staggeringly wordy moment.

Secondly, we never had any contact number or address for John Brown. 'But how will we be able to tell you if the game's off?' Frank Uber asked. In a particularly long response for John, he replied in true film star style, 'I'll contact you', which he did. In the lead up to potentially rain-affected games, John would frequently call Frank from a phone box for updates.

Thirdly, he never travelled to or from games with anyone, and always parked his car – an ageing silver Datsun - about a quarter mile from the ground.

Puzzled by this, one day he was secretly followed back to his car after the game. It turned out that not offering a lift home to anyone was not necessarily ignorant, but because there was simply no room for a passenger as the car was packed full of toilet rolls. Not definitive proof of witness protection, but surely pretty close.

And the final piece of evidence: suddenly John just disappeared. One Saturday he didn't show up, which was entirely unlike him. We were a bit worried, but had no way of checking he was OK, or if - as an OG historian of the time noted - he had been on the wrong end of the 'Chicago typewriter'.[16] Fortunately, the next mid-week Frank found a note from John under his door. He was becoming almost verbose: *'Sorry. I have moved on and will not be back. John.'*

He was never seen again. Which was a pity: I really liked him. He was probably the only OG I knew who never at any point talked shite.

Frank Uber was finally a convert to the Witness Protection Scheme speculation on John. Ever

---

[16] At the time, no-one had the slightest idea what this phrase meant – just that it was unlikely to be good. As it turns out it is a reference to the 1920s heyday of gangsters in the USA. At one point, there were so many tommy guns in the Windy City with their characteristic 'rat-a-tat' sound, that this became known as the 'Chicago typewriter'. I only found this out recently through the brilliant Smithsonian TV channel; looking back, it was remarkably apt observation on the potential fate of John Brown.

an opportunist, he then suggested that perhaps we could advertise for other people on the scheme to join the OGs. Fortunately, some of our legally trained teammates explained that this might not be practical.

Delusion

This a cross cutting and supporting reason for why people joined the OGs, normally combining with one or more of the above. In summary, some people played under the delusion that they were much better at cricket than was objectively the case. It is actually a puzzle why this is so prevalent; in many ways cricket should be one of the least suitable games for the deluded. The way cricket scores are recorded is brutally clear, individual, and unavoidable. *'T.D. Smart bowled Thatcher 0'*, or *'T.D. Smart 2 overs, no wickets, 4 wides, 25 runs conceded'* are examples of recorded history that are very difficult to spin positively.

Contrast with a sport such as football – a team can win a game 1-0, with only one recorded goal scorer. But many of the other 10 in the team have played well, and it is by no means certain the goal scorer has been the best player. So post-match reviews leave much scope for subjective analysis on individual performances, leading to many pub brawls.[17]

Cricket has no such place to hide, though this has not meant OGs haven't tried over the years. For example, I have heard batsmen seriously claim they made 'a good three', or that they 'bowled a great over that only went for 20 runs'. My favourite, however, is the claim once made of a 'critical piece of fielding that saved four runs'. This in fact was an easy dropped catch 25 yards from the boundary rope.

A healthy cadre of 'delusionists' is vital to cricket selectors, bringing hopeless players back again and again. It is important that this is not equated with stupidity: many of the OG standouts in delusion were our academics.

Increased personal prestige and attractiveness

On reflection, there are no recorded examples of this as a reason why someone joined the OGs. I have no idea why. But a list with 10 things on it is sort of neat.

---

[17] Football is of course not immune from this type of delusion: it is just harder to sustain. An example would be a midfielder, that teammates had forgotten was on the park, claiming he 'did a lot of important and selfless running off the ball'.

Chapter 4 – England Our England

'It is never difficult to distinguish between a Scotsman with a grievance and a ray of sunshine.'

P.G. Wodehouse

This chapter addresses a key existential question which in a way explains something about my obsession: 'Why do Scottish people support England at cricket?'

One afternoon in the late summer of 2005, I received two phone calls – both from Scottish women friends working in London. It was the last day of the famous Ashes series that had gripped England for months and had even appeared in the Scottish news! England were successfully batting to avoid defeat, led by a brilliant 150 from Kevin Pietersen. The Ashes were returning to the home of cricket after 18 years - a long time in which England considered simple defeats as a light relief from humiliations. Workplaces across the land had downed tools for the afternoon, and TVs had been wheeled in for staff to watch the final denouement.

I was also watching in Glasgow – alone of course, as colleagues again pitied my 'cricket problem' and continued working. The phone calls I received in quick succession were virtually identical, and in the classic 'phone a friend' mode. 'Tommy, why on earth are we supporting England at cricket? You are the only person I have ever met that might know the answer to this.' It was not really a compliment, and not an easy question. It requires a little bit of background context.

Scottish and English people have an interesting relationship within the same small island. It is mainly a healthy rivalry, with many of the attitudes on both sides typical of a geographic context in which one adjacent country is much larger than the other.[18] At worst, some Scots appear to have a serious chip on their shoulder: this is countered by an English extreme of dismissive arrogance. Normally it is good humoured, but it involves an asymmetrical view of respective sporting achievement.

A few years ago, I went into the centre of Glasgow on a Saturday morning. It was a lovely earlier summer's day, and there was a happy holiday-type atmosphere. The streets were busy with many people in strange attire for Scotland's largest city –

---

[18] I suspect a similar tension may be in play if a slim Bermudian woman marries one of her island's male international cricket team.

German football tops, and t-shirts emblazoned with the letters 'ABE'. Less common was the extraordinary sight of a tubby middle-aged man sporting nothing other than a tight pair of shorts and a first world war German helmet, spike and all. Were Germany in town to play Scotland? Not at all; this behaviour was triggered by a sporting event taking place over eight thousand miles away that had nothing to do with Scotland.[19] Germany was playing England in the last 16 of the 2010 football World Cup finals in South Africa.[20] The people of Glasgow were 'showing their colours'. This was not out of any great love of Germany, with whom we've had a few scraps in the past; rather the clue is ABE – 'ANYONE BUT ENGLAND'.

It is not reciprocated. One of the hardest conversations I have had a few times is when an English person asks directly why, whilst they would want a Scottish team to do well, we want anyone to beat England? In truth, there is no convincing answer to this, but it is deeply inbred in many Scots. A common backtracking response is that it's not England or the players we don't like, it's the commentators – always exaggerating how good

---

[19] Scotland had once again opted out of this football finals tournament.
[20] England lost the game comfortably, and were involved in another famous World Cup finals 'ball over the line off the crossbar' incident. This time it didn't go so well for them.

England are and banging on relentlessly about their sole World Cup success in 1966.

Now, Scots would never do this – claiming, for example, that a late winner in Andorra is a harbinger of national football recovery. And of course, Glasgow Celtic fans seldom mention 1967, the sole Scottish triumph in the European Cup (now the Champions League).[21]

I do not think Scots should *necessarily* support England in sport. One argument is that we are all part of the same United Kingdom. Before June 2016, this was certainly a stronger argument, but the Brexit referendum result that forces Scotland out of Europe against its clearly expressed wishes has, I suspect, ended the 'United' bit.[22] Time will tell if this fracture is subsequently confirmed constitutionally. England's unfortunate habit of being conned by posh boy idiots and the likes of Liz Truss,[23] will certainly keep the torch of independence alight. How hard these folks

---

[21] This is not in any way to detract from the outstanding achievement of Celtic's 'Lisbon Lions' led by the legendary Jock Stein. 10 of the 11 Celtic players were born in Glasgow, the other in Saltcoats on the Ayrshire coast. Think on that when you are watching the next Champions League final! It is for me Scotland's finest ever sporting achievement.

[22] I understand lots of people in England think Brexit means that they have 'got their country back'. I used to have an old auntie who regularly 'got her piles back'. I suspect she got the less painful deal.

23 Liz Truss used to excruciatingly mention she was briefly at school in Paisley as part of her leadership credentials. (She clearly did not have any others.) It is surely the town's darkest hour, and as a born and bred 'buddie', I can only apologise.

work - with their hopefully diminishing band of toadies - to ensure Britain will in no sense remain 'Great'.[24]

So why is cricket different? On the spot, the answer I gave on that famous 2005 afternoon was a garbled version of the first reason below. Now, with more time to reflect, I suggest two main reasons: the English cricket team isn't English; and Australia.

The Cricket World Cup final of 2019 is one of the greatest matches ever played. After many hours of gladiatorial battle, the two sides ended up with exactly the same score – a tie. The game went to a super over – just six balls when each team tried to score as many runs as possible. This was also a tie.

Consider the final moments. Batsmen Ben Stokes (born in Christchurch, New Zealand) plays a wonderful innings, bowler Jofra Archer (born in Bridgetown, Barbados) bowls a wonderful over, fielder Jason Roy (born in Durban, South Africa) runs out the opposing batsmen to secure victory, and captain Eoin Morgan (born in Dublin, Ireland) lifts the trophy. ENGLAND had beaten New Zealand to win the World Cup.[25]

---

[24] I wonder, if Scotland does become independent, if we will erect a statue of Boris Johnson in Edinburgh by way of thanks. It could perhaps be commissioned alongside the rather bigger one of Arlene Forster required in Belfast by Irish republicans.

It was great day for cricket. Unbelievably, Tory Boy Jacob Rees-Mogg claimed it somehow vindicated the Brexit shit show. This is not made up! 'Moggy'[26] was once again showcasing the deep research and thinking characteristic of all his utterances. It is not a particularly recent phenomenon; Kevin Pietersen, the hero of the 2005 Ashes final day, was born in Pietermaritzburg, South Africa. The composition of an English touring side to his native land was once so packed with compatriots it led to a joke at the time: 'Where do the English cricket team stay when they tour South Africa? Their mum and dads!'

The story of the World Cup final has wider implications over why Scots support England at cricket. Quite simply, one of these heroics to win the game could have been by someone born in Glasgow, or Edinburgh, or Paisley. Scotland does not qualify to play 'test' cricket – the highest form of the game.[27] On the few occasions a Scot has been good enough to play at this level they have required to play for England. Though infrequent in number, in my time

---

[25] England had won on a technical rule that I or anyone else I knew had never heard of. The Cup should have been shared. The graciousness of New Zealand captain Kane Williamson in defeat did his small country proud.

[26] I pondered whether to use this nickname, as 'moggy' is also name for cats. These have always struck me as likeable animals, not known to destroy people's lives for personal greed. Sorry cats.

[27] Scotland does have a one-day cricket team, and play England from time to time in this format. The last game was in 2018, when of course Scotland won. In many ways, England's world cup win the next year was a sort of consolation.

two England captains have only been eligible through Scottish connections – Tony Greig[28] and Mike Denness. [29]   As a consequence, my and many other young Scottish cricketers' dreams were of scoring the winning runs for 'England'.

The reasons people from non-UK countries end up playing for England are more complicated. For me, it adds to the sport, and hopefully dampens some of the more unpleasant forms of nationalism. (Assuming you are, of course, just a little better informed than Moggy, which isn't normally a great challenge.) If it strengthens your side, then fine, and I have no problem at all with the range of reasons why players choose to adopt England as their cricketing nation. With a massive injection of talent and dedication, it could have been me!

And, of course, we as Scots are not immune from such chicanery to strengthen sporting teams. A few years back, I remember an interview with an

[28] The late Tony Greig is best remembered for his contribution to motivational psychology. He qualified to play for England through a Scottish grandfather but was to all intents and purposes a white South African. In 1976, when apartheid in South Africa was at its high point, by now England captain Greig foolishly said he aimed to make the touring West Indian side 'grovel'. A surprisingly well motivated West Indian side subsequently thrashed England.

[29] Born in Bellshill near Glasgow, Mike Denness was not the most successful England captain. He was unfortunate to be leading the side when the legendary Australian fast bowling duo of Dennis Lillee and Jeff Thomson were in their pomp. In these days, Australia appeared less interested in beating the English team than in trying to kill them.

English Premier League footballer selected to play for the Scottish national team, based on the discovery his grandmother had once eaten haggis. He was asked if he'd ever been to Glasgow's famous Hampden Park. In a broad south of England accent, he famously replied, 'To be honest, mate, I've never been to Scotland!' More recently, there are unconfirmed claims a new Scottish striker, when asked to sing the national anthem before a game, instinctively burst into *Waltzing Matilda*.

So to recap: the first and main reason Scottish people support the English team at cricket is because it is not exclusively 'English'. The second reason is Australia.

In test cricket, the longest and most intense rivalry is between England and Australia.[30] Every two years or so the bragging rights in this contest at Test Match level are determined over five games in 'The Ashes' series. It is a riveting watch, so much so that when played in England every four years, the entire period is referred to by cricket lovers as an 'Ashes summer'.

---

[30] The only test match rivalry which compares with the intensity of The Ashes is India v Pakistan. Sadly, due to political tensions between the countries, test games between the countries have not been possible in recent years. It is a real pity.

Brought up as an England supporter, I was brainwashed into a dislike of the fiercest rival. This was not really necessary or impressive, but with the Australian cricket team it was surprisingly easy. Always admired, they were never likeable. Series after series they produced fearsome warriors, hugely talented and determined to win at all costs. This would extend to stretching every rule, and maximum intimidation of their opponents. They believed, and were often correct, that they could psychologically wear down England by finding the 'soft underbelly' of the poms when the going got tough.

A key part of this was the Australians' undisputed place as the champion exponents of the cricketing 'tactic' known as 'sledging'. This may surprise many people less familiar with the game. As you watch this 'gentleman's' sport from a distance, you probably have no idea about some of the soft-spoken discourse underway between the batsmen and close fielders. This is entirely based on breaking the batsmen's concentration by getting them worried or angry – and thereby prompting a bad shot.

At its most mundane this can include simple direct stuff like, 'You're shite!' or, 'This next ball is removing your head.' But it is the more subtle stuff that works best, such as suggestions on the inappropriate activities of the batsman's wife whilst he is at the cricket, whether he definitely locked the back door when leaving the house, or whether he left the upstairs bath on.

Though the Australians excel at this, it is prevalent to some degree at most levels of cricket. In my early playing days at senior level, I was once subjected to this in a local Paisley derby. We were holding on for a draw, and whilst batting I was surrounded by much older opposing players plotting my demise. As the bowler approached, in true Corinthian style one foe whispered, 'I hear your girlfriend's shagging half the school.' Naïve as I was, I replied, 'I don't have a girlfriend.' But I was so pumped up because he thought I might, I batted beautifully, and we avoided defeat.

The Australian sledging seldom backfired like this, and it contributed to embedding Scots support for England; true to rivalry and loyalty across sport, it created the myth of an evil 'enemy'. The Australians did one other really annoying thing – they kept winning. How I hated them!

But whilst this may explain supporting England when playing Australia, it doesn't justify supporting them against everyone. Which I, and many Scots, do. The illogicality of this is at its most extreme when England play the West Indies.

For me, it is impossible not to love West Indian cricket. This has been influenced by the fact that for most of my cricket playing years, they were by far the best team in the world. But it was, and is, because of more than that. It is always an exciting brand of cricket: lightning-quick bowlers, magnificent and flamboyant fast scoring batsmen, and outstanding athletic fielding.

It is also cricket with a smile. The great West Indian teams always suggested they weren't 'grinding out' victories (as per Australia), they were enjoying every minute. Over the years the smiles of players such as Viv Richards became embedded in my memory of cricket. And this tradition continues today when watching the likes of the 'Universe Boss' Chris Gayle, and Dwayne Bravo.

The politics of West Indian cricket is also important. As a concept, the 'West Indies' only really exists as a cricket team. This brings together a number of independent Caribbean islands, often some geographical distance apart. Avoiding inter-island rivalry has not always been easy, and it has required some critical leaders to build a united team – with none greater than Guyanese Clive Lloyd. In many ways, the cricket team has become the 'brand' of these islands, and lifted the area's profile. Cricket is also a focal point in the fightback against the legacy of slavery and racial oppression. Beating England at cricket has always been, and still is, a 'political' statement.

In the summer of 2020, a West Indian team bravely took the risk of touring England to enable the reintroduction of cricket following the initial wave of Covid-19. The side was led by their very impressive captain, Barbadian Jason Holder. This tour also coincided with the continually rising profile of the 'Black Lives Matter' movement. Taken together, it was an emotionally charged time, and the West Indies team doing well became a part of this.

On paper, and in English conditions, England looked too strong. But in a gripping first test match, which ebbed and flowed throughout, the West Indies got home for an exceptional last day victory. It was brilliant to watch, and the celebrations at the end joyous. Major Caribbean political leaders sent Jason Holder a message congratulating the side.

But for me the West Indies' dramatic win was not the main highlight of the five-day test match. It was edged out by a truly outstanding Sky Sports podcast on BLM. Fronted by the great Michael Holding and former English women cricket international Ebony Rainford-Brent,[31] it is one of the most emotional pieces of TV I have seen. Simply talking to camera, these two exceptionally gifted and strong people relayed their personal experiences of being on the wrong end of racism. Both at points broke down, and I challenge anyone watching it not to do likewise. It brought home again the reality that if you have not personally experienced racism, you struggle to fully understand it. If you have not watched this, I beg you to track it down and do so - and share with everyone you have ever known.

So, given my tribute to all things West Indies, who was I supporting through all this? England. Come the second test, having rejoiced in the West Indies' opening win, I then bizarrely sat down to cheer on the home side, who subsequently won the series 2-1.

Confused? Me too!

In this chapter I have tried in some way to explain why people in Scotland support England at cricket. If you remain unconvinced, worry not: in re-reading the above, so do I. But it is too late for me to change now, and with many fellow Scots I will go on hoping that someday an *Englishman* will emulate the Irish and lift the cricket 50-over World Cup![32]

---

[31] Ebony is hugely knowledgeable about cricket, very funny, and plays the drums. She is also staggeringly attractive, and – although I have no evidence as such - believe she is an enthusiastic follower of St. Mirren Football Club. After my wife of course, 'Ebbs' is my fantasy woman.

---

[32] It should be noted that the English women's team have no such outstanding aspiration. For example, captain Heather Knight lifted the 50-over World Cup trophy after a thrilling win against India in 2018. Heather was born in Rochdale, in the greatest English cricketing county of Lancashire.

Chapter 5 – If Writers were Players

'I tend to think that cricket is the greatest thing that God created on earth. Certainly greater than sex, although sex isn't too bad either.'

Harold Pinter

As you read on, you will quickly realise that these memoirs are largely of a low-level nature. They cover many of the more basic aspects of the human experience: excessive drinking, defecation in all its forms, marital infidelity, fraud, religious intolerance, and individual delusions. On this basis, I am very proud of my humble Rabelaisian attempts to stand on the shoulders of Geoffrey Chaucer.

But before delving into the underworld, this chapter considers one of the few occasions when we at least aspired to a higher literary plain.

This did not apply to many OGs, and certainly not our coarse seam bowler Evan Tron, who once famously commented pre-match, 'If I see anyone ever bringing one of these fucken big papers [aka broadsheets] into this dressing room again, I'll wipe my arse with it. And then I'll put it back in their bag!'

But the OGs, like many club cricket teams, was an eclectic band: a broad church indeed.

I like to imagine a relationship between cricket and literature – which has always been important to me. If it is not your bag, skip this chapter. Don't worry, we get fully into the gutter shortly.

In 1986, in a moment of strange ambition, a short OG August tour was arranged. It was not the most physically testing cricket touring schedule, and did not demand any requirements to rest key players. The pre-tour schedule was short, clear and surprisingly well written in the style of Hemingway:

Friday – drive to Nottingham. A 'light supper' on arrival. Drink. Late night game of French Cricket in hotel bar (host permitting).

Saturday – get drunk at day three of the England v New Zealand Test Match at Trent Bridge. Curry (if allowed access).

Sunday - get drunk at day four of the England v New Zealand Test Match. Curry (if still allowed access). Late night team talk.

Monday – 20 over bounce game against a team in an outlying Nottinghamshire village, courtesy of a contact wicketkeeper 'Red Can' had made in a Birmingham pub earlier in the year.

Though incidental to this particularly narrative, for accuracy it should be noted that this game never actually took place. After a futile three hour drive around scenic rural Nottinghamshire, we concluded that the opposing team did not exist. Only then, did Red Can admit that his Birmingham conversation had been very late on a rugby night out, and that looking back he realised that no actual dates for this match had ever been discussed. On the upside, it meant that we returned from the tour unbeaten.

Through no particular planning, my carload on the journey down contained probably the best the OGs could muster in terms of a cultural powerhouse. This consisted of myself, surprisingly well-read burly all-rounder Jamie Grip, generally big-brained Trevor Stone, and our guest tourer Lionel Degree, a cricket-mad Professor of Literature at the University of Glasgow.

I need now to quickly digress to establish my shaky credentials in this company.

During four uninspiring years studying political philosophy, I quickly tired of: John Locke (well-meaning but short on humour); Thomas Hobbes (nasty bastard); John Rawls (boring bastard); and to a lesser degree Niccolo Machiavelli (clever bastard).

In my despair, a friend gave me a copy of Henry Miller's *Tropic of Cancer*. Now, this book has sort of divided people, but one thing is for sure: Henry, unlike Rawlsey Boy, was not boring. I loved it, and it led me to a decisive new approach to academia. Accepting that you have to read something at university, why not embark on a reading schedule with one sole criteria: it had nothing to with your course?

The outcome as I left my alma mater was predictable, but it led me to a feast of literature. Unlike school, where I scraped an English Higher on the old adage of 'just read the back cover and say you found the book enigmatic', I became an obsessive reader. At a rebellious age, the pull of reading anything other than what I was expected to was truly liberating.

Many a day I sat – inside in winter, and outside on at least four days each summer – devouring the classics. This was assisted by something I think I may have misunderstood from Ernest Hemingway - that you had to do this whilst drinking huge volumes of red wine. More specifically, the sweet Italian wine, Valpolicella. ('Cool as fuck,' I often remarked to bemused friends).

Fortunately, this was in the early 1980s, and Margaret Thatcher's enlightened policies had led to economic chaos and uncertainty. Hard as it was to witness the destruction of jobs and communities, poverty, and the decimation of all liberal values, there was at least one upside. Due to recession, in a small shop in Glasgow's Woodlands Road you could get a litre and a half of Valpolicella for £2.99.

My nascent, and still unfulfilled, career as a literary critic was launched. Book after book I would devour, beverage in hand. For reasons some have suggested are linked to this, my memories of how books start are much stronger than of how they end.

As a young romantic, I had my fantasies and challenges. Central to these was how by time travel I could have got the scants off Tess of the d'Urbervilles, or found Emma Bovary's 8,000 francs to stop her suicide (plot spoiler). But lest you dismiss me as over ambitious, even in my youth I realised the best I could hope for with Dorothea Casaubon[33] was a flirtatious, intense, but ultimately platonic outcome.

So, there I was with the OGs' cultural elite in the car on our 'tour' to Nottingham. Inevitably, in the troubled Britain of the 1980s, we hit road works at Penrith, two hours south of Glasgow. Even in a carload of such erudition, conversation was drying up.

And then Jamie Grip had perhaps his finest moment as an OG by asking, 'Why don't we pick our best XI of famous writers based on how they would play cricket?'

I did not initially see the genius of his suggestion, with my immediate response, 'Are the wine gums done already?'

But after a short silence, Professor Lionel Degree, of whom we were all in awe,[34] spoke.

'Not a bad idea at all, Jamie.'

Six hours later, after furious debate, we arrived in Nottingham with our team, batting order, and coaching notes.

---

[33] The leading character in George Eliot's *Middlemarch*. A magnificent book, but a big unit. At least six litres' worth of Valpolicella.

[34] I should clarify this was only in a literature context. As a cricketer, he fitted well into the OGs by being very ordinary. That said, Professor Degree could articulate the many weaknesses in his game much better than the rest of us.

George Orwell (Captain): Rock solid opener, moral compass of side. Technically sound if unspectacular shot maker. Capable of adapting to all formats. Very good at reading game and thinking ahead. Back up spin option, but unlikely to be used much. Some fitness doubts.

Guy de Maupassant: More attractive and flamboyant than Orwell, with game more suited to limited over format. But good foil in maintaining run rate if Orwell gets bogged down, or overthinks the situation.

Gustave Flaubert: Technically the most gifted batsman in the side, with exceptionally precise shot selection, and guaranteed to contribute lots of runs. Greatly admired and valued by his teammates, and very difficult to get out. Huge positive influence over Maupassant if at the crease together. Strong and intense first slip.

F. Scott Fitzgerald: Most attractive batsman to watch by some margin. At his best outstanding in a Goweresque mode, and capable of outrageous improvisation. Even better in limited over format. Inconsistent and potential injury concerns. Requires close management. Also prone to self doubt and requiring significant sport psychologist inputs. Off-field behaviour demands careful monitoring.

Jane Austen: Fluent and reliable with bat, and solid medium pace bowler. A joy to watch and a fine cover point. Not so strong in limited over format, and very chatty in field. Guaranteed to keep dressing room morale high with outrageous stories about the opposition.

Henry Miller: Recognised as a wild card and controversial selection. Untested at test level, but his unconventional and direct approach may pay dividends. May require to go down order if early wickets lost. Erratic leg spin option. Important to keep away from Fitzgerald off the field.

Charles Dickens (wicketkeeper): Mr. Reliable behind the stumps with bags of experience. Fantastic motivator and all-round team man. Extremely stubborn but desperately slow scoring batsmen, taking a very long time to build an innings. Bat above Miller if early collapse, and a key man if playing out time for a draw.

Emily Bronte: Young mystery spinner and hard-hitting lower order bat. Plays particularly well at high altitude grounds. At her best unplayable, with some surprising maturity in her game given her age and lack of experience. Fast and speedy outfielder. But her commitment and enthusiasm suggest potential burn out, and a foreshortened career.

George Eliot: Quality left arm over medium quick seamer and solid lower order batsman. Ever reliable, but again can potentially get bogged down when batting. As with Hardy can bowl long spells, and together they form a great bowling balance with the potentially exceptional but temperamental Burns.

Thomas Hardy: Reliable medium quick seamer. Capable of long spells, and always asking questions of the batsmen. Particularly effective on small, rural grounds. May be lacking a bit of variety in his delivery options, and don't expect any quick runs from his batting down the order. Likely to be a stalwart in the team for years, but unlikely to be 'Mr Laughs' in the dressing room.

Rabbie Burns: Flamboyant, unpredictable and lightning fast-paced bowler. A completely uncoached Scottish genius, capable of some inexplicable match winning performances. But need to keep an eye on how close he wants to field to some of his female teammates.

It is truly a powerful and well-balanced line up.

Inevitably, some very good options, despite having many recognised strengths, failed to make the team. Below are the assessment notes I recorded all those years ago.

Ernest Hemingway: can bat on his day, but flatters to deceive, and has too many shocking off days. Potential on-field clashes with Fitzgerald. Could also bore on tour.

Charlotte Bronte – too similar to her sister. Difficult to find a place for both Brontes in the team. Potential replacement if Emily's career comes to a premature halt.

Knut Hamsun: Sorry to miss out on the Norwegian's mystery spin, and stubborn late middle order batting. But as an overt Nazi sympathiser, provoked hostility amongst some of the selection panel, and could lead to boycotts from other players. May not secure visa for some overseas tours.[35]

Tom Sharpe: On his day magnificent, but perhaps out his depth at this level. More in contention for one day side.

William Boyd: The mid-1980s just a bit early to make the side. But huge potential, and certainly one for the future. Captaincy potential longer term, if Orwell's fitness deteriorates further.

---

[35] Hamsun's novel *Mysteries* is one of my favourite books. What the fuck happened, Knut?

Sebastian Faulks and Julian Barnes: See William Boyd above.

Dorothy Richardson: Very slow scorer, may be brought back into consideration if they reintroduce timeless test matches.

Marcel Proust: Technically very gifted, but not a team player. Desperately slow scorer, and unlikely to be available for overseas tours. Unreliable, sleeps in a lot, and injury prone.

Sir Pelham Grenville (P.G.) Wodehouse: Any time he wasted playing rather than writing about cricket would be criminal.

Nancy Mitford: Controversially left out due to identity confusion with her many sisters, some of whose social activities and choices of spouse concerned the selectors.[36]

Now, let's get back to Chaucer.

---

[36] If you get nothing else out of this book, and you have not already done so, read Nancy's *The Pursuit of Love.* You will thank me. Her sisters had an unusual choice in men; one married British fascist leader Oswald Moseley, and another apparently tried to cop off with Hitler.

PART 2 – HEROES ALL

Chapter 6 – One man and his dog

'The girls they will give it of course
But they give with such force
That it gives you remorse
Oh, the dogs, they give nothing at all
They just lift a leg
As they watch it end.'

The Girls and the Dogs – Scott Walker

If you were to come across one of the few OG team photographs from the latter part of the 20th century, you may detect a clue as to why the name 'Graeme Kilbride' does not appear often in these memoirs. This is despite Graeme being an unreliable top order batsman and an OG stalwart with many years of service (if not runs). Also despite him being the source of more entertainment than he was probably ever aware of.

Look closely as you scroll the picture, and your gaze will land on a chunky, friendly, red faced, and bulbous-nosed figure. You may think, 'I know him! That can't be right, an obscure Scottish cricket team in the mid-1980s?' A further clue is perhaps needed: think not of the OGs, but of the halcyon days of your youth in Yellowstone Park. Quite simply Graeme Kilbride was Yogi Bear. The likeness was so astonishing, a good lawyer may have secured breach of copyright. The legend that was 'Yogi' was easily born.

To explain how completely the name Graeme Kilbride was airbrushed from history, I need to quickly explain the nature of a traditional cricket scorebook. It is a matter of some honour and tradition that your name is listed with full initials. For example, the scorebook names of some famous players over the years have been: I.T. Botham; A.P.E Knott; I.V.A. Richards, and R.G.D. Willis.[37]

'G.R.S. Kilbride' would have had quite a good ring to it, but despite his pleadings, Graeme was only ever registered in the score book as 'Y. Ogi'.

As it happens, this sometimes had a strange and accidental side effect. Many club cricket teams often hire an overseas 'professional'[38] from stronger

---

[37] A fine fast bowler and excellent pundit, Bob Willis actually added the third name of 'Dylan' to his original name in tribute to his musical hero Bob Dylan. He died in late 2019 and is sadly missed. This gesture truly confirms he was a class act.

[38] For more background, professionals or 'pros' are players paid to come in and win games single-handedly for very poor amateur teams. To my knowledge, they did not offer free sexual services.

cricketing parts of the world. On the very odd occasion that 'Y. Ogi' did enough to merit mention in cricket scores section of local papers, some opposing teams became concerned we had made an expensive overseas signing swoop. Once the game started, it very quickly became apparent that this was not the explanation of 'Y. Ogi.'

Yogi did not come alone: the full experience involved his latest love interest Moira, and his errant dog Bounty. A beautiful chocolate brown Labrador, referenced as a 'pup' for approaching 10 years, Bounty had deep undiagnosed – and probably un-diagnosable – behavioural issues. He may also be the only pup in history to cost a sports team a league title.

At the beginning of season 1988, a late winter double signing scoop by Frank Uber in Milngavie's Multan Tandoori had significantly strengthened our squad. The transfer fee was apparently a guaranteed weekly visit by the Uber family to the 'all you can eat' Tuesday buffet. With the new additions, although a perennial Glasgow League second division side, OG promotion to the top league seemed in sight. Moreover, with his early season form diminishing further, Alf Gibbs had finally decided to call stumps on his distinguished career. His final reasoning, however, surprised many, with the extraordinary claim he had twice been wrongly given out, caught off his wooden-sounding replacement hip.

By mid-August our title dream was in sight. Only a heavy defeat against our arch rivals Renfrew stood in our way. But as the key home clash with Renfrew approached, our squad was decimated by a combination of holidays, the recurrence of marital discord, and a large Bengali society wedding in Milngavie.

We were weakened, and even a desperate attempt to entice Alf back out of retirement failed. A 'tidy' lottery win, and some surprising foreign trips with the strangely named Minty Clinch – an equestrian themed Johnstone stripper – had rejuvenated him. He happily told us to 'fuck right off', still apparently bitter about the undisguised mirth his retirement explanation had provoked in our ranks.

'Can we not go back again and see if Mike Gibb can play?' spinmeister Trevor Stone suggested at a crisis selection meeting. 'Otherwise, Frank may have to get the camper van back out at the school games, and the police are getting increasingly twitchy about that sort of stuff.' No-one said it as such, but the phrase 'political correctness gone mad' was all but telepathically communicated.

Mike had formerly been the star player of a rival team that had folded two years earlier. This source had delivered vocal seamer Evan Tron, who still kept in touch with Mike, and regularly reported he was desperate to play.

'It's his wife Sheila. She's very house proud and likes Mike around at weekends; apparently he's very good with his hands. She also hates cricket - thinks it is boring, incomprehensible, and that nothing ever happens. Bizarre woman!'

'Can we not sell it to her as a lovely summer's day out and forget the actual game? Tron, your wife knows her; we could try and get some of the other wives down – glass of bubbly, nice picnic, wee chat, top up the tan sort of thing.' Legally trained Trevor Stone stood out as the team thinker and strategist.

'As long as they still make the mid-innings tea for us as well.'

'Not now, Tron.'

'What's she like anyway?' Trevor continued.

'She's actually OK, just a bit quiet and reserved, and very proud and self-conscious about her appearance.'

'Give me their number and leave it with me.'

Trevor's learning and charm paid off, announcing on late Thursday, 'He's in, and Sheila's coming too. Tron and his wife are picking them up, so she can have a few scoops, which will probably relax her.'

In Mike we had secured a fine batsman and – as we all knew from bitter experience – an infuriatingly slow but effective bowler of huge in-dippers.[39]

We were ready; the humbling of Renfrew was at hand; the champagne was chilling.

Match day duly arrived as a glorious late summer afternoon. The ground looked in superb shape, and the home support had grown to unprecedented double figures. (It has to be admitted this was short term, as it transpired a group of local young women had in fact got lost on the way to an outdoor yoga session.)

Sheila Gibb was much nicer than feared. An attractive women attired in a beautiful and expensive yellow polka dot dress, she was shy but friendly and

---

[39] A bowling style that can get batsmen - who are not nearly as good as they think they are - out.

seemed to easily bond with the other wives. We also wisely kept her well apart from some of the less savoury social characters in our team.

The toss was won, and we elected to bat on a good pitch. Mike opened with the ever-reliable Donald Track, and in good time we were 50 without loss.[40] Renfrew were visibly losing heart as the day heated up.

What could possibly go wrong? Enter stage left – Bounty the wonder dog!

The wives and next few batsmen had positioned themselves on gently sloping grass in front of the clubhouse. Given the weather, it was truly idyllic - calm and soft with the gentle sound of cricket in the distance. A second bottle of chilled white Piat d'Or was close to completion, supported by a surprisingly impressive suite of canapés. Much of this effort was for Sheila, and it was working; she was relaxed, laughing, and slightly pissed. Mike's status as an OG was secured for years to come. We weren't just going up; we were going to make a serious impression on the top league.

---

[40] A good start.

Sheila even felt comfortable enough to confirm she really didn't like cricket: 'A lot of silly ageing men excited about nothing.' It was taken in good part, and surprisingly, a number of the other wives for the first time agreed it was 'all a bit sad'.

Bounty was a mischievous dog that craved attention. Seizing Yogi and Moira's absence for an unexplained joint trip to the toilets, the lure of the canapés and the company proved too much, and he charged towards the sitting spectating group.

With the exception of Sheila, everyone was aware of Bounty's annoying behaviour. But he was just a daft dog and was in turns indulged and vaguely ignored. Sheila looked more concerned.

"I'm not very comfortable with dogs, and sort of allergic to them.'

'Don't worry,' Mrs Tron reassured her. 'We'll get Yogi to take him away when he reappears.'

But Yogi's absence extended for an inexplicable length of time.

Now it is a strange phenomenon, but dogs and cats seem to have an obsessive attraction to people who are allergic to them. And Bounty continued to pester, and almost isolate Sheila. Her attempts to gently shoo him away increased in force, only serving to further excite the beast. Eventually Sheila's patience failed, and she swiped hard at Bounty with a loud cry of, 'Oh just fuck off!'

It was too much for the excited mutt, who froze for a second before pissing long and forcibly all over Sheila's lovely new and expensive yellow polka dot frock.

A lasting second of silence ensued, and then even the cricket game stopped in response to Sheila's outburst.

Yogi – roused by the noise – appeared from the clubhouse doing up his trousers.

'For fuck's sake, get your fucken dog under control,' yelled Trevor Stone. He looked as incensed at his failed strategy as the mortgage and pension-holding Tories who thought Liz Truss had some cracking ideas for the economy.

Yogi, surprisingly for such a normally slow-witted man, immediately grasped the situation. He charged at Bounty who was now next to an amazed cover point.[41]

'COME HERE YOU WEE BASTARD!' yelled Yogi.

But, as we have established, Bounty was no normal dog, and probably quite a bit below average dog IQ. He seemed incapable of distinguishing between being in serious trouble, and someone wanting to play with him.

Eighteen-stone Yogi, by now a colour of puce never before seen, was invited to get near enough Bounty to swipe a kick, and then just in time, the dog sprinted off 20 yards and invited his master to continue the game. This was repeated several times as Yogi and Bounty weaved between the frozen Renfrew fielders.

The game had now stopped for some period. Eventually, the panting dog was apprehended by the square leg umpire and marched to Moira, who was now also finished 'toilet duties'.

'I think it might be an idea to put the dog in the car,' the umpire whispered. These remain some of the wisest words I have ever heard.

But Bounty's panting compared not a jot to the condition Yogi was now in. Unfit, overweight,

---

[41] A fielding position, normally key to stopping runs rather than dogs.

over 40, and probably post-coital, his normally florid features now seemed almost illuminated. He finally made it back to the dressing room, head bowed, past a group of silently hostile teammates and spouses.

By this time, Sheila had already left the ground, sobbing violently and accompanied by Mrs. Tron, who had generously offered to take her home.

'She'll probably just go and put a new dress on and come back,' reflected tail-ender Hugo McFarlane, aka 'Denzil'. This was characteristic of Denzil's impressively consistent record of never saying or doing a sensible thing in 20 years as an OG, and why he merits his own chapter later in these chronicles.

For the record, neither I – nor any other OG – saw Sheila again until 2001. Obviously Mike did. But I understand that, partly due to this incident, he no longer sees much of her anymore either.

Despite these distractions, the title decider still had to be played out. It was then that the true cricket ramifications of 'Bountygate' began to unfold. Mike, who had viewed the spectacle from the non-striker's end, understandably lost focus and was quickly out to an outrageous shot, characterised by complete indifference. As he entered the dressing room, he threw his bat in disgust. 'Well that's my fucken cricketing days over for good!' Accidentally, the bat split on impact with a sink, and a sliver of willow flicked into the eye of burly all-rounder Jamie Grip, who was getting ready to bat. It was agony, but Mike generously offered to drop Jamie at casualty in his taxi home to appease Sheila.

Jamie's painful screaming led me and a number of teammates to go into the dressing room. After failing to console him, another thought crossed my mind: 'Where's Yogi?' He had not been seen since his march of shame back to the clubhouse.

Quickly I located him slumped in a shower cubicle. He was not looking good, and a very odd colour. Utility fielder Dr. Gordon Bronze was summoned, and suggested he better get checked out at A&E. This was remarkably sage advice; having long hinted he was a GP, we later we found out Gordon's doctorate was actually in marketing.

Fortunately – for all, I suspect, other than Bounty – Yogi made a swift recovery. But Mike never returned, and burly Jamie lost temporary sight in his left eye for two weeks.

Down to eight demoralised and shocked men, we succumbed to 94 all out. Deprived of two front line bowlers, Renfrew easily knocked off the runs for a nine wicket victory.[42] It gave them a one point lead in the league. Being Scotland, it then rained from mid-August till the following April, and our bitterest rivals were champions.

Can a dog lose a cricket league? I rest my case.

---

[42] A pumping, or heavy defeat.

Chapter 7 – Denzil

'Each time I find myself flat on this face
I pick myself up and get back in the race.'

Frank Sinatra - That's Life

The West Indian Malcolm Denzil Marshall was one of the finest fast bowlers in test match history.[43] It is a tragedy that after an outstanding career, he died way too young at just 41 years of age. His skill was matched by commitment and bravery, having once batted in a test match with a broken arm. He was, and remains, a hero to cricket worshippers worldwide.

Every aspiring young fast bowler wanted to be Malcolm Marshall – to hurl the ball with ferocious pace at a terrified batsman. Importantly, Malcolm had one key advantage over these likely lads – an unerring ability consistently to land the ball in the right place. Malcolm's legacy in inspiring young cricketers was and is positive; it has motivated many to become much better players. But there are always

---

[43] Marshall was one of the 1980s West Indies test match team generally recognised as the best of all time. Australians, please take note.

exceptions, and this leads me to re-introduce OG Hugo McFarlane – aka Denzil.

Hugo was not a great cricketer. In one sense he was an 'all-rounder', as in all-round shite. The only positive thing I could ever say about his extremely restricted batting skills is that they were significantly better than his 'ability' as a bowler. This was blatantly apparent to all but one human being – the man himself. Even someone with absolutely no knowledge of cricket would, after a few minutes of witnessing Hugo in the practice nets, wonder how his bowling related to the guy with a wooden thing 22 yards away.

'But daddy,' I can imagine a watching youngster saying, 'does the ball not have to go somewhere near the man with the stick if he is meant to try and hit it?' Out of the mouths of babes we have hopefully established a reasonable picture of Hugo as a bowler.

Hugo was never allowed to bowl in games; it would have been difficult to see how he could have concluded an over. (Question for rule buffs: after 15 consecutive wides, can an umpire call it void?)[44] But

---

[44] A 'wide' is ball so badly directed the batsman cannot get near it. A penalty run is awarded, and the ball requires to be bowled again. OG records indicate that 5 in 6 of the balls Denzil bowled in the nets were wides. Reproduced in a match situation, he would have needed to have bowled on average 36 balls to

in practice sessions he was his ever optimistic and energetic self, hurling the ball anywhere off a ridiculously long run up.

It was all but inevitable that one night the ever self-unaware Hugo would ask his OG colleagues, 'Do you think I might be as fast as Malcolm Marshall?' I do not feel any need to describe the reaction. It was so ridiculous a question, leading to thoughts of rebadging Hugo as 'Malcolm'. But it seemed too obvious, and a more subtle suggestion of nicknaming him after the great bowler's little-known middle name won the day.

Whether by accident or design, this also fitted perfectly with the legendary slow-witted character from the TV sitcom 'Only Fools and Horses'.

'Denzil' was born. It stuck, and from here on he shall be known.

As a player making a contribution to the team's cricketing fortunes, Denzil would not merit a footnote in these chronicles. But as a character, who brought so much joy to his teammates, he was truly a superstar.

---

complete a legitimate 6 ball over. Even in the long late June nights of a Scottish summer, no cricket match could ever have been completed in this scenario.

Born as the only child of a wealthy family, years of expensive public schooling had graduated Denzil with a first in idiocy. Prior to his christening as Denzil, he often appeared on the team sheet as 'Bertie Wooster's Idiot Brother'.[45] But he had many compensating positives: good looks; posh voice; money; expensive cars; charm; an unwavering confidence; and no moral values whatsoever. In short, the full package of qualities for a Tory MP.

He was relentlessly positive, and to his credit never bore a grudge, though this may have been because he appeared unable to retain any information.

Whilst never I suspect having made a single contribution to the country's GDP, he always appeared to have huge amounts of money. In these days it was always hard cash. Commonly, as the post-game cry of 'match fees' was announced by the ever-unpopular treasurer, Denzil would delve into a wallet stuffed with notes of a colour many of us had never seen, and offering his 50 pence, ask, 'Have you change of a fifty?' (This, it should be remembered, was the 1980s, when £50 could secure you a deposit on a small house in an 'up and coming area', and virtually all of Greenock.)[46]

---

[45] 'B.W.I. Brother' – see chapter 4.
[46] This line is entirely for the entertainment of St. Mirren supporters.

Denzil claimed that this surfeit of money was because, unlike us other losers, he was an entrepreneur. (Someone must have given him this word.) When questioned, his precise business interests were very vague, and ever changing. They included a scheme to sell vulnerable old people in wealthy areas life insurance policies that didn't actually exist. Denzil's explanation that 'They all look pretty healthy to me,' did not immediately suggest a robust business plan.

Perhaps an even more surprising development was a subsequent claim while getting changed for a match that he had established a new venture 'building computers'.

'What, like IBM?' all-rounder Jim Track inquired.

'Yes, that sort of thing,' replied Denzil.

There was a slight pause, as everyone began to ponder how many ways this didn't quite add up.

'What sort of size of company is it?' Trevor Stone asked, as I suspect he shaped up a forensic prosecution case.

'Well, it's just me at present, but I've got a girl from one of those schemes starting on Monday. By the way, she's a real honey.'

Fortunately for Denzil, the umpires called us to the field, and he avoided having to respond to Trevor's rather obvious but devastating follow up question, 'Do you actually know anything about computers?'

Two weeks later, Denzil's grab for a share of the lucrative computer market was over. The 'real honey' had been let go, after an unspecified altercation between Denzil and her rugby playing fiancé. Other back-up recruits failed to materialise, and Denzil, in a rare moment of reality, admitted to some cash flow difficulties. Amstrad computers continued to thrive without competition from what we can only imagine would have come to market as the 'Denzil' PC.

Many other ludicrous business ventures ensued, all with complete failure. Due to Denzil's high rolling business dynamism, I suspect his very wealthy father was becoming not so very wealthy, confirming the old dictum that the easiest way to have a small fortune is to start with a big one.

As mentioned, Denzil's cricketing abilities were very limited. And when he fully integrated these with his stupidity, the results were even more catastrophic. It was an example of when the concept of the 'sum of the parts' could seriously backfire.

In our second venture to a major cup final, defeat loomed. Chasing a good total, we had managed to claw our way back into contention, but our perilous hopes can no better be summed up than by the fact Denzil had come to the crease. Confident as ever, he strode to the wicket with his new, expensive bat - rumoured to be worth more than many of our cars.

With one wicket left, all our hopes lay with Jim Track, who had worked hard to reach fifty and was batting well. We needed 12 to win, and in his current form Jim could see us home. But Denzil would now be on strike,[47] and he had to stay in or all was lost.

As he walked out, our captain Jamie Grip bellowed out an instruction that perhaps contradicted

---

[47] At any time in a cricket match, two batsmen are at the crease. But obviously only one can face each ball. This batsman is said to be 'on strike'. You can only alter this if a batsman scores one or three runs, or the over (six balls normally) is completed. To maximise your chances, you logically want the better of the two batsmen on strike as much as possible. You would, if it could possibly be avoided, never want Denzil on strike.

100 years of positive thinking literature. 'Now remember Denzil, you CAN'T bat!'

'Right, Denzil, just get me back on strike. Get anything on the ball, and we'll run,' Jim somewhat more positively advised.

Denzil nodded, but his next comment was in retrospect a worrying portent: 'What do you make of my new bat?'

'Lovely, but just get me on strike,' a more worried Jim replied.

The bowler rolled in, and as they say in cricketing parlance, 'put it in the slot'. Denzil wielded his gleaming bat, and in the most outrageous and irresponsible shot of the day, hit the ball cleanly out of the ground.

Our reaction was genuinely mixed. Six runs (doubling Denzil's total for the season) meant we only needed another six to win. But it was also the stupidest shot imaginable in the circumstances.

Jim Track was similarly conflicted. 'Great shot, Denzil, but just calm down. Defend the next one and we'll get a quick single.'

Denzil barely listened, his eyes still fixed on the trajectory of the ball's journey. He then looked down. 'Some bat! This is all I've been lacking.'

Jim walked back to the non-striker's end, increasingly concerned.

The bowler was rattled and under pressure. A hopeless number 11 had just hit him for a huge six, and the game was well and truly back in the balance. But he had one thing in his armoury that the opposing batsman lacked: a brain.

Up he ran, same delivery but much slower. Denzil failed to calculate that this meant the ball would arrive at him a crucial few milliseconds later. He once again launched his bat at the ball and was swung off his feet, as the ball had not yet travelled half way to him. As he fell, he looked back and watched it hit his middle stump.

Game over. We had lost the match and the cup by five runs. Jim Track remained 56 not out.[48] Jim and Denzil returned to a subdued and angry dressing room. We were bitterly disappointed. No-

---

[48] As two batsmen have to be at the crease at any time, if 10 of the 11 players are out, the whole innings is over. Despite the team being 'all out' one batsman left is recorded as 'not out', but also has to leave the field. Hopefully, to non-cricket lovers, this helps to better justify the physical assault perpetrated on Denzil.

one could even look at them. But true to form, the ever unaware Denzil broke the silence: 'Did you see that six I hit?'

To this day, none of us are proud about the physical damage we collectively administered to him. Fortunately, he only required outpatient treatment. And being Denzil, all was forgiven (or forgotten) by the next match.

Unsurprisingly, Denzil also had a chequered and troubled love life. And one of these episodes again contributed to cricketing misfortune for the OGs, and ended my only stint as club captain.

In the tradition of 'Someone's got to do it sometime,' I was elevated to this important leadership role. It was going to be a tough year ahead: we had gained promotion to the top division, but historically always struggled at this level. Consistent with our low expectations, the last game of the season arrived as a 'loser takes nothing' relegation showdown away at Prestwick. It was going to be a tough game, but we had a chance.

As captain, you had the 'honour' of picking the team. But this was in fact the thankless and demanding task of finding 11 broadly able-bodied people to turn up, and then hoping at least some of them could play cricket.

In this context, I had a puzzling phone call on the Friday night before the game.

"Hi, it's Mary here, I hope you don't mind me calling you at home.'

'Mary?'

At this point, I noticed my wife looking at me suspiciously from a nearby sofa.

'Yes, from the cricket.'

'The cricket?'

'Yes, you know, I used to do the scorebook.'

'Oh yes, Mary who used to do the scorebook at the cricket,' I said loudly for the benefit of my increasingly interested wife. This was meant to appease her: it didn't.

'I'll not keep you. I just wanted to check if Hugo is playing tomorrow.'

'Hugo? Oh, you mean Denzil. Yes, he is.'

'And it's away at Prestwick?'

'Yes.'

'Thanks. I'll see you then. Bye.'

As I put the phone down, my completely puzzled look was matched by a look from my wife swaying between a similar curiosity, and something much darker and hostile.

'Who the fuck is Mary, and why is she phoning you on a Friday night?'

It demanded an answer then, and it is also necessary now to provide readers with the background to a chain of events that ultimately led to the OGs' relegation.

A few years earlier at my first game for the OGs, I noticed an unusual sight. Amongst a mass of largely overweight men not blessed by the Gods of aesthetic beauty, sat a lovely, serene young woman. She did not seem to be with anyone, and was barely noticed or acknowledged.

'Who is that?' I finally asked.

'Oh, that's Mary, she does the book.'

For readers unfamiliar with cricket, this refers to someone who painstakingly records all individual and collective batting and bowling scores, alongside the overall outcome of the game. The 'book' provides the details of who is winning, and who is playing well or badly. But as most cricketers would admit, the main function of 'doing the book' is to ensure we can bore each other to eternity in pubs on the arcane details of past games.[49]

It is not a particularly easy thing to do, is not exciting, is not paid, and normally has to be done by one of the players. It takes quite a bit of time to learn, and requires concentration for up to eight hours.

So why was young, attractive Mary giving up every sunny summer Saturday to this entirely unappealing task?

Perhaps it is reflective of a dark part of my nature, but I initially concluded that there had to be something wrong with her. I decided to investigate.

'Hello - Mary - my - name - is – Tommy,' I said slowly and loudly, in a way that would have patronised a five-year-old.

---

[49] It is not possible to overstate this observation.

'Hi Tommy, I heard you were joining. There are great hopes you may be able to improve the team. Could be a tough game today, but if we win the toss, I reckon we'll be OK.'

Entirely normal, clearly knowledgeable about cricket, and even more attractive in conversation, it quickly transpired that this was an engaging and intelligent young woman. I could find no chink in her armour.

I was puzzled.

But once again, drink came to the rescue. After the game – a victory – we predictably went to the pub to celebrate. Mary joined us, lovelier than ever, and after a few pints, my traditional lack of tact and directness came to the fore.

'Mary, what are you doing here?'

Silence. Donald Track uncharacteristically scowled at me and made an unmistakable throat cutting sign for me to desist from continuing my enquiries.

'Sorry, bit badly put. What I meant was, given your many charms, have you nowhere else to go on this fair summer's evening?' Somehow, I thought this type of olde English parlance may help dig me out.

'Not now Hugo's gone up the road. He is often quite tired after the cricket, and just wants to go home.'

I looked suitably bemused.

'I'm not quite with you. Why does this matter?'

'Well, before the wedding, he's quite traditional, and doesn't like staying over. So, if he heads off, I often just stay with the rest of the cricket guys. Don't really fancy going out on my own.'

I should perhaps better explain my problem with this conversation. Not only had Hugo not acknowledged his 'fiancée' Mary at any point in the day, I had attended his wedding earlier in the year to the glamorous Michelle.

I had truly found the chink in Mary - and it was quite a chunky chink. Unlike apparently everyone else, she was utterly unaware Hugo was already married. Coming to the cricket to score was one of the few occasions she could be guaranteed to be in his company.

How, you may ask, could this clever and attractive woman be so stupid as to commit herself to the feckless Denzil? I can only respond that people voted for Brexit and Donald Trump: they can get things badly wrong.

Thankfully, Mary did become aware of the technical challenges in progressing her engagement to its normal conclusion – but only a week before the big day. Denzil's initial attempt to deflect by claiming he was sorry, but he had doubled booked, eventually led to the whole thing coming out.

Mary was devastated for a while, but I and many others reflected on the wisdom of Garth Brooks when he sang, 'Sometimes I thank God for unanswered prayers.' Less poetically, she had not so much dodged a bullet as a Trident missile.

This was a few years before Mary's phone call on the night before the Prestwick game. But it is important causal context.

It transpired that twice in the period of their engagement, Mary had lent her 'husband to be' significant sums of money. This was invested in one of his many business ventures, which meant it lasted slightly longer than flushing it down the toilet.

'So what?' thought Mary as she made her fateful miscalculations. 'Our futures are bound together, Hugo wouldn't do anything irresponsible.' Love is indeed blind.

This money had, of course, never been paid back. Mary, a nice, decent, and unforceful schoolteacher, contacted Denzil from time to time and was repeatedly ensured it was on its way.

The situation lasted until Mary finally met the true love or her life, Gerry, a joiner from the challenging Glasgow area of Possilpark. As they began their plans for a wedding that would actually take place, Mary mentioned that this sum of money was outstanding.

Gerry's response was considerably less sanguine than Mary's. As a tough working-class boy and the offspring of a Labour councillor and a local gangster,[50] his annoyance that Mary was fairly owed the money was inflamed as she filled him in on the nature of Denzil's character.

'If that fucken rich ponce thinks he can fuck off with our money, he needs to think again,' was one of his more printable observations.

---

[50] For clarity, this refers to two parents.

'But any time I ask him to give me back the money, he just agrees, and then doesn't show up with it.'

'Then we should go to him and be a little more insistent.' Gerry was beginning to feel quite excited.

'But I have no idea where he lives, and he doesn't work.'

Gerry narrowed his eyes and thought for a moment. 'But he plays cricket. Find out the next game, and if he's in the team.'

'We'll need to move quick,' Mary noted. 'The season is just about finished.'

So, after some necessary detail, hopefully the significance of Mary's random phone call to me – years after she had stopped doing the book - falls into place.

It was a tense match at Prestwick's lovely seaside ground. The picturesque and affluent town of Prestwick on one side; the beach and Firth of Clyde on the other.

We batted first, and put up a reasonable, but by no means unbeatable, score. Prestwick were showing nerves in reply given the high stakes of the game, and our 'runs on the board'[51] looked as if they might carry the day.

There was no margin in the game – every run counted. Focus and concentration were key.

Suddenly, a white van screeched into the car park and ground to a halt. Gerry appeared from the driving seat, followed by a somewhat sheepish Mary. Two sizeable chaps jumped out of the back, equipped with what were unmistakably items of Gerry's joinery equipment. My initial reflection was that, in a tight spot, you would rather hope these guys were on your side.

'McFarlane!' bellowed Gerry. 'Payback time!'

Fortuitously, the only unambiguously correct decision I made in my captaincy career had positioned Denzil in a fielding position deep on the far side of the ground. In hunting terms, it at least gave the fox a chance.

---

[51] An observation, from many years of cricketing history, is that it can be harder to chase down a defined score. When you bat first, your only aim is to score as many as possible but batting second you know exactly how many are needed to win. Known as 'scoreboard pressure' this can trigger nerves for the batsmen as the winning margin gets close. This latter phenomenon affected the OGs frequently - over the years it was strangely less observable in our opponents.

Oblivious to any cricketing etiquette, Gerry and his associates charged across the field waving some pretty serious pieces of equipment aloft. But Denzil was not slow, and had built up good fitness from many similar 'running away from creditors' scenarios. He was over the wall in a flash and heading across the beach. Laden with armoury, Gerry's vigilantes struggled to keep up. In a few minutes, all were out of sight – heading up the coast, or out to sea.

Eventually, the game recommenced. Missing a fielder, and losing focus, we went down to a narrow defeat and relegation.

Denzil never returned that evening. And the white van remained. In the sombre dressing room atmosphere, we looked with bemusement at Denzil's untouched clothing. We couldn't wait all night, so in the end we decided to leave it in case he came back. But just before we closed the dressing room door, an inspired Evan Tron announced, 'Give me a minute.' He quickly reappeared holding Denzil's ever-bulging wallet aloft.

'This may help us ease the pain of demotion tonight,' he triumphantly declared.

Despite these setbacks, Denzil's relentless romantic instincts continued. Michelle had quickly departed the scene, realising that her HNC in Health and Beauty put her well above Denzil's intellectual league.

But superficial charm and the impression of wealth are clearly irresistible to some of the female of the species. Wedding bells were again in the air: Denzil had successfully wooed Susanne, the only child of a self-made Ayrshire parvenu. It was considered a 'good match' – the continuation of a rags-to-riches journey by the family heiress marrying into the upper middle classes.

A huge 'society' wedding was arranged. Nuptials in a quaint and historic village church, followed by a lavish reception in one of Ayrshire's most prestigious hotels. The OGs were invited in force, and in the context of unlimited free drink, answered the call in full. It was a great night, and in the well-meaning bonhomie often generated by a wedding, we tried to put aside our many concerns on Denzil and wished the new couple well.

How we cheered as they headed off in a flurry of confetti to a luxury three-week honeymoon in the Seychelles.

'Fair play to Denzil. He's landed on his feet for sure,' quipped the normally cynical Tron.

Denzil missed the rest of the season on his holiday idyll. His next outing was consequently our annual Christmas get together. Memorably, he was sporting a new aquamarine coloured blazer.

'So, how's married life?' I innocently asked him.

In a classic Denzil detachment from reality moment, he replied, 'Oh you mean with Susanne? That's all over. The formal divorce was concluded in November.'

No response was really possible, so he continued.

'You see, what you guys didn't know was that I was formally declared bankrupt the week before the wedding. Susanne's dad Charlie found out but didn't let on. As the huge wedding was all paid for, and many relatives were coming from all over the world, he kept quiet, and thought it would be even more embarrassing to cancel.'

'Equally, the honeymoon was non-refundable. Despite being minted, Charlie's as tight as nun's chuff, so he wasn't going to let that go.'

'Must have been a tense holiday?'

'Not really, I didn't know at the time. Susanne did, but fair play to her we still had a cracking break.'

'So how did it end?'

'Well on the plane back, after few glasses of bubbly, Susanne looked deep into my eyes, and in what seemed a romantic moment, said she had something important to tell me.

'Hold on a minute, I just need to go for a piss, I told her.' (A wonderfully unnecessary Dickensian detail that Denzil was good at.)

'As I stood in the toilet, I wondered what was coming. Could she know she was pregnant already?

'Jauntily, I strolled back to my seat.

'So what is it darling?
'She told me everything, and that our married life would end with all haste. Her father would pick

her up at the airport, and she would never see me again. The family lawyers would be in touch.'

This tale certainly got our festive celebration off to a flier. A high bar had been set for the future discussion topics.

'But hold on a minute,' legal ace Trevor Stone interjected. 'I suspect if the divorce was to avoid Susanne's money getting swallowed up in your bankruptcy, legally it's not that straightforward. I still think they should have just stopped the wedding.'

Pause, and then a thoughtful Trevor continued, 'And another thing, in Scots law I don't think you could be formally divorced between a marriage in late August and the same November. Even if consensual, just not possible.'

'But Susanne's dad is not stupid. He had it all worked out,' replied Denzil.

'How so?'

'Well, to avoid a serious kicking from some of his associates, I agreed to sign a statement that on the night of our wedding I told Susanne I was 100% gay, and that the marriage was never consummated.

Apparently on this basis, you can get it quickly annulled.

'Anyway enough of all this serious stuff, did I tell you I am getting a new bat for next season?'

Denzil had many faults. I am forever grateful he was part of my life.

Chapter 8 - Building an Innings

'The ordinary batsman, whose average always pans out at the end of the season between the twenties and thirties, does not understand the whirl of mixed sensations which the really incompetent cricketer experiences on the rare occasions that he does notch a few.'

PG Wodehouse

This short chapter is based on a recurrent theme of these memoirs – personal delusion. Cricket is good at this.

It showcases Gavin Bland, who in truth was not an important OG or regular player. But confirming Andy Warhol's observation, he at least thought he had his 'five minutes of fame'.

'It was a bit of a green top,[52] not easy early on – just a matter of survival. Oh, and I'll have a lager as you're at the bar.'

---

[52] A 'green top' is a damp wicket with too much grass, which tends to be slow and difficult to bat on. It favours the bowlers. The wicket is the main piece of grass cricket is played on, this can also be called the 'pitch', the 'strip' or the

Why had I not agreed to stay with the guys who had volunteered to bring in the boundary markers and close up the clubhouse? One-on-one with Gavin for God knows how long. Karma indeed!

Gavin was the local postman. A dangerously visible occupation in the village home[53] of the OGs. He was quickly spotted and snapped up by Frank Uber. 'If he can post letters, he's bound to be a bit of a player,' was typical of Frank's enthusiasm, which at times followed no known logic. On this, and sadly many occasions, he could not have been more wrong.

'So how long ago was this innings?'

'14th July 1982.' It was now the summer of 1994.

12 years on you may think a reminiscence of a more recent performance would have been appropriate. But I suspect you may already be ahead of me.

'track'. A 'wicket' can also refer to a batsman getting out, or the three pieces of wood at each end. These pieces of wood are also called the 'poles', the 'sticks', or the 'timbers'. The opposite of a 'green top' is arguably a 'shirt front'. Maybe this footnote thing is not such a good idea after all.
[53] These chronicles cover a period when the OGs moved between playing in Paisley and the wealthy village of Kilmacolm.

Again, let me digress for a moment.

West Indian Sir Vivian Richards – the 'master blaster' – is the greatest batsman I have ever seen. I once had the privilege to see him bat at The Oval in London. I can still feel the hairs rise on the back of my neck thinking of the reception he received from the huge West Indian support. Normally, you would not hear this for a batsman returning with a double hundred.[54] This roar was for him only walking out to bat.

He strolled from the pavilion with the strut and swagger of an African prince, confident he and his teammates would once again put England to the sword. This mattered: England at the time were far from the second-best team in the world, but as commented many years later in the brilliant documentary 'Fire in Babylon', this was 'master versus slave'.

For the many West Indians in the ground, it was payback time for the relentless racism they experienced in England in the 1980s. A more modern acronym, now popular in the Glasgow area, may have helped communicate their feelings: GIRFUY.[55]

---

[54] A very good individual score. Only a handful of times in OGs history did the entire team manage to score over 200.

Viv duly delivered, hitting the English bowlers to most parts of London in another crushing Caribbean victory.

What, you may well ask, has this to do with Gavin Bland?

It aims to provide context and relativity: if all the batsmen that have ever played cricket were put on spectrum from good to bad, Gavin would be as far from Viv as possible. The two literally bookmark the range.

I cannot ever remember Gavin – a lower middle order batsman and specialist third man – ever actually scoring a run. There had been a disputed leg bye[56] in an early season friendly, but some accused Gavin of doctoring the book after the game. Quite simply, he did not seem to have any mechanism whereby the ball could leave the square. His batting technique could best be described as crab like, and it was not always entirely clear where his bat was. And he never ever seemed to get any better.

Curiously, neither I - nor anyone I have raised this with - was present at the game on 14th July 1982.

---

[55] 'Get It Right Fucken Up Ye'.
[56] A run which does not hit the bat but the batsmen's leg, for which he does not get personal credit. Very poor players try and claim it hit the bat to augment their meagre totals. Good players are embarrassed that they missed the ball.

Research also indicates it was actually a Wednesday. Given this, and that Gavin is the sole source of evidence of this innings, purist historians and legal types may have some verification issues.

Gavin returned to his story.

I desperately looked around; still no-one else. I am forced into a sort of 'carry on' look.

'I think I'd been put up the order as a blocker:[57] hard to get out, but perhaps not with quite as many strokes as some others who may in the circumstances have played some inappropriately flamboyant shots.'

I suspected this was a dig at me, but declined to respond directly. I also decided not to mention that reports suggested the two normal openers and number three had been held up in a traffic jam, and that by start time only seven OGs were present, including the 10 and 11-year-old daughters of the club skipper.

'The two opening bowlers were quick and moving the ball sideways.[58] I have to admit I played and missed a few times,[59] though the opposing team

---

[57] i.e., shite.
[58] Good for bowlers, not for batters.
[59] In Gavin's case, missing a ball that is not hitting the wicket by a significant margin.

seemed barely to notice. At that point it was just a question of nicking off the odd one and two.

'But then I sensed the shine going off the ball, and a hint of tiredness. I opened up a bit, and in turn saw off both opening bowlers. The last thing I wanted then was to let the inferior third seamer off the hook with a few quiet overs, and took him on straightaway. I could feel his confidence going immediately.

'They had no option but to turn to spin.[60] It was not turning much (though normally they have to bounce for that to happen). I was seeing it like a football, and the field spread far and wide. It was controlled aggression – big shots followed by quick singles to tire the fielders further.

'I could see we had some stroke players in the hutch, so as we passed the 25 over mark, decided to just go for it.

'Inevitably I finally holed out in the deep.[61] But I had laid the platform, and with some powerful late order hitting, we ended with a total of 109.'[62]

---

[60] At this level of cricket, a bowling style for people physically unable to bowl any faster.

[61] In Gavin's case, caught out by an opposing fielder standing 10 yards away.

[62] A low overall team total, and very unusual if an individual player has made a significant personal contribution. In a way that it transpires Gavin Bland had not.

I have to say that Gavin's narrative had strangely caught my attention. Could his game really have reached this peak that I had missed? The problem was that low overall team total; how badly had his teammates let him down?

'So how many did you end up with?'

'13.'[63]

With my mouth shaping some astonished response, fortunately for both of us, the opposing team appeared for a post-match pint.

1994 proved to be Gavin's last year as an OG. The following winter, after an unspecified misdemeanour, he was 'moved sideways' to a new post round in the east end of Glasgow. There his fortunes deteriorated further, as he was caught stealing benefit giros. After it became clear only a guilty verdict was possible, Gavin remained true to form, and seeking the limelight, claimed he'd probably misappropriated approaching a million pounds. The actual figure was £11,009.

---

[63] A very ordinary individual score, that would normally take a very short time to amass.

Chapter 9 – El Presidente

'Follow, follow!'

Traditional football song in some parts of Glasgow

Any set of chronicles on the OGs would be criminally negligent without dedicating space to long term club President Archie Ranger.

This is a difficult chapter to write as trying to do justice to Archie is a huge challenge. I am consistently beset with doubts as to whether it is possible to fully capture him. He was such an extreme and outrageous character that anything written almost seems like understatement.

I'll start with a few words, and then fill in some detail. Loud; robust; florid; passionate; inebriated; unmissable; unedited; Presbyterian; kind.

Archie and Frank Uber were the two biggest cricket fans I ever met. But Archie recognised that it was way too narrow to experience life's rich tapestry through this single lens: there were other sports. Two of these directly impacted on a typical OGs' summer: until late May, and again from early August, football. In the middle period, this supporting role was assumed by 'the bowlin''.

Now, as most readers would expect, the majority of OGs' football allegiances lay with Paisley's world renowned local team St. Mirren.[64] This included all sensible playing and support staff. But the proximity of Glasgow was always a problem, and there was some leakage of glory hunters and people with additional support needs to the two puzzlingly named 'Glasgow Giants' – Celtic and Rangers.

As anyone familiar with Scottish football will be aware, it has historically and unhelpfully been dominated by these two clubs – annually a classic two horse race. However, in the early 2000s, this imbalance and lack of competition was somewhat exacerbated when one of these two horses committed suicide.

I digress here with the unashamed justification of personal indulgence and enjoyment.

---

[64] At the time of writing, St. Mirren have won the Scottish Cup three times – in 1926, 1959 and 1987. I realise if you are reading this in, say, ten years' time you may be thinking, 'I never realised that before their recent domination of the competition, St. Mirren had not won the cup since the previous century.'

The key point is that Archie Ranger was well named, and – counterbalancing his many other positives – he was a passionate supporter of the deceased horse. But this particularly story predated this demise, and Rangers, through a shrewd strategic combination of tax evasion and spending money they did not have, were still competing for major domestic honours.

What, you may ask, has all this got to do with the OGs? I will explain.

Throughout the cricket season, Archie's attendance at one of his two other sporting loves preceded making his way to the latest OGs game. This had two consequences. Firstly, the outcome of the football or bowls impacted markedly on Archie's mood. Secondly, either activity provided ample opportunity for Archie to get started on the gin.[65] Combined, it meant Archie's arrival at the cricket was characterised by being very drunk (always), and very angry (sometimes).

Archie's entrance smashed the normally sedate and quiet ambience of a club cricket game. An initial bellowing of 'OGs!' would normally be his introductory pitch. From wherever in the field you

---

[65] A strong alcoholic beverage.

were bowling, fielding or batting, it was never necessary to look round for verification of who it was. The volume was extraordinary. Though it has never been entirely proven, anyone – OG or opponent – would strongly support the thesis Archie swallowed a microphone in his young days, and that it subsequently proved impossible to dislodge from his throat.

Catching up on the cricket score, an OG doing well was initially lavished with praise. This was genuine, but it limited Archie's range. His real oratory skills flourished to much greater effect on the opposition. This could be general, but more commonly identified one individual prey – the wildebeest separated from the herd by a hungry and drunken lion.

The attack began and was sustained. It included, but was by no means limited to, cricketing prowess (or otherwise). Whether through extensive research or simple guess work, all aspects of the victim's life to this point were in scope. It also seemed to suggest more Roman Catholics born out of wedlock played cricket than was I suspect the case.

Looking back, I reckon Archie's robust interventions did the OGs' cricketing fortunes more harm than good. Often, he targeted the opposition's best player, with the aim of knocking him off his game. Being good players, however, this simply inspired them. We were consequently often on the wrong end of some outstanding and strangely committed performances by these opponents.

But one of Archie's greatest strengths was that, rolling on the clock four hours, he would be slumped over the club bar, quadruple gin in one hand, and his other arm draped around the object of his earlier vitriol. By this time, Archie had ensured this opponent was well on the way to equalling his drunken incoherence. 'BFFL', to use the parlance of a different era. Strangely, all earlier and very public observations on this player – his cricketing ability, sexuality, wife's fidelity, religion, mother and sister's income sources, physical condition – were all laughingly forgotten. Until, of course, the rematch, when Archie would roll out the same old tune. Most of his victims did not seem to care; over time the achievement of becoming the opposition focus of Archie's ire became a badge of pride.

I have hopefully by now managed to communicate that the consumption of industrial quantities of alcohol was the axis around which Archie's life orbited. Any OG of the time will have their favourite stories on this, and I will pick out one of mine.

As mentioned elsewhere, we twice reached the final of a major cup competition. This demanded the strangest of all OG gatherings – an actual selection meeting, and one where the sole criterion was cricketing ability. The privileged cabal given this task was Archie, myself, and fellow all-rounder Jim Track. It was tricky: for the first time in living memory, we required to leave out an actual cricketer. Serious intent and detailed analysis were clearly needed.

On the Thursday before the big game, we duly convened at Archie's comfortable if somewhat dated bungalow. It was the first and only time I was ever in his house, and I found the apparent domestic normality difficult to square with Archie's outrageous lifestyle.

'This is the biggest game in our history,' Archie started. 'We need to get this right tonight. Every man will count.'

Jim and I nodded in solemn agreement.

'OK, probably best to start with a drink.'

'I was kind of thinking that me and Jim should maybe lay off it, in preparation for the match,' I timidly suggested.

'Nonsense!' roared Archie. 'The game's not till Sunday, remember. A drink will steady your nerves.'

Without waiting (or more accurately allowing) for a reply Archie left the room, and returned with a clearly prepared hostess trolley laden with more alcohol than would be required for a mid-sized wedding involving two heavy-drinking Scottish and Irish families. It was groaning with every conceivable option – except of course beer, which Archie always considered a 'soft drink'. All our needs were catered for: ice, lemon, and impressive crystal glasses.

The meeting began. Initially many options were considered in detail. In fact, it was quite a high quality and informed discussion. Scenario planning if we lost early wickets; cover for an injury or off day for a front-line bowler; fielding strategies; rain interruptions reducing overs per side; how to keep Yogi's dog Bounty from disrupting proceedings.

But the lure of the hostess trolley gradually took its toll. Archie decided the concept of tonic in gin was overrated, and we all decided that the garish aubergine coloured liqueur brought back from a distant Algarve holiday was a much better mixer option. As a consequence, we lost discipline and memory.

Somehow, I made it home. Awoken early by an anxious call from Denzil, without any introduction he asked, 'Am I in?' Recovering composure, I replied, 'Leave it with me, I'll call you back.'

Over the course of the morning, I managed to contact both Jim and Archie, and we had to confess none of us could remember the final team selection. Archie had been writing it down but suspected he may have mistaken this yellow Post-it note for a crisp late in the evening. This was before his morning ablutions, but his offer that he may still be able to retrieve it was not taken up.

Realising the embarrassment of our predicament, we agreed one of us would just make up the team that morning. No-one will ever know if it was the same team we decided in the selection meeting, but we won the final!

Everything about Archie suggested that rather dated concept, 'bachelor'. His entire lifestyle suited this, and it was very difficult to see how anyone could possibly envisage Archie as 'love's young dream'.

But many years on, Archie wrong footed us all when it emerged that the 'full flood of masculine passion' had not abated, and that he had 'a woman in Knightswood' (a suburb of Glasgow). Moreover, this was a long-standing relationship which had produced a now grown-up daughter.

Looking back, we did begin to piece together the post-match nights when Archie, a litre of gin to the good and unable to finish his madras, would suddenly say he had to go. The mental image of a woman patiently waiting for him – with potentially amorous intent – as he staggered in after eight hot hours of sweat and abuse, outrageously drunk, and covered in curry, is not an easy one to eradicate. But as the great Bob Dylan penned, 'True love tends to forget.'

And strangely, though I'll never now have the chance to ask Archie, I suspect this was a love affair.

Archie had also been a solid player in his day, although his sartorial reputation for never being able to fully button up his trousers perhaps limited what he might otherwise have achieved in the game. He also became a well-respected international umpire, and his overall knowledge of the game was hugely impressive.

Archie's innings ended a few years ago. Given his lifestyle, making it to his mid-70s baffles medical science. He enjoyed life to the end and died peacefully after a short illness. If there is a hereafter, let's hope they got some notice and pre-ordered a few tankers of gin.

His funeral on a cold and bright early January day did him proud. A huge turnout thronged the Paisley Crematorium, including an army of former OGs, and many of the long-standing objects of his abuse from sister clubs. His coffin was led in, appropriately adorned with two cricket bats, and a Rangers top. The eulogy noted his life-long passions – sport and drinking. I would imagine any aspiring stand-up comedian dying on his arse would be very jealous about the ease with which the celebrant brought the house down with the simple line, 'I understand Archie liked a drink.' He also mentioned how one of the great highlights of Archie's life was the OGs winning the Small Clubs Cup. 20 years or more on, it was only then that I realised the full importance of what we had achieved that day.

The coffin slid into eternity to the musical refrain of a song about the Duckworth Lewis method: this is not an obscure form of birth control, but a formula that determines the result of rain affected cricket games.

As we slowly shuffled out of the crematorium, was I the only one who heard a single loud and ghostly cry of 'OGs' as we passed into the daylight?

We looked at each other in the car park; there was only one final tribute we could pay Archie. 'Pub anyone?'

Archie Ranger was someone I fundamentally disagreed with on most non cricket related things – but he was a good man whom I miss. He was never dull. I look forward to sharing a few large gins with him in the great beyond.

Chapter 10 – The Wedding Party

'Show me a hero, and I'll write you a tragedy.'

F. Scott Fitzgerald

The build-up

Surprising as it may seem, ineffective batsman Yogi's darkest hour for the OGs was not the championship-losing events of the game against Renfrew chronicled earlier. Without question there was a monumentally more awful incident at the culmination of his weekend of wedding celebrations the following year.

'Bittersweet news, guys,' he announced one showery Saturday as we waited for the rain to abate and the game to start. 'Moira and I have decided to get married. You are all invited.'

This was not perhaps greeted with quite the enthusiasm and interest that could have been expected. It was not the first time Yogi had pledged a lifelong commitment to an eternal soulmate. In fact, he may have been married more times than his score had topped 30 and appeared in the local papers.

The curiosity from Yogi's news was more in the 'bittersweet' introduction. This requires some background on his wife-to-be. Moira was a kind and decent person, but she had a number of issues and characteristics that also placed her in the 'unusual' category. One was that she spoke very quietly and very slowly, which was at times a bit spooky. She also only spoke to Yogi and used him as the conduit for all communications. It was never clear why this was the case and covered even the most trivial exchanges.

For example, 'Graeme [real name only ever used by Moira], can you ask Jamie to move a little to his right? His stomach is blocking my view.'

Yogi then duly advanced this information, though we had already heard it, and Jamie was by now breathing in.

But the key defining aspect of Moira was her mysterious health issues. For as long as any of us could remember, Moira had always been 'unwell' in a completely undefined way. This demonstrated itself in two key ways.

Firstly, I suspect Moira became very adept at 'looking' rather than 'being' ill. I do not think this was deliberate as such, but it became a sort of personal USP.

Secondly, Yogi's comments were littered with hints such as:

'You know with the way things are with Moira.'

'It's not been a good week for Moira.'

'We're always a bit restricted, given Moira's circumstance.'

'We try and make the most of every day.'

I should clarify, given how much more we appreciate it nowadays, this was not reference to a mental health issue which we were completely insensitive to (though sadly the 1980s OGs would have been). It was always clear this was primarily some physical ailment. With an audience, Yogi could often be seen helping Moira out of the car. For a woman in her late 30s, this was not good.

But it was never articulated what was actually wrong with Moira, though it was hinted as being of a degenerative and ultimately terminal nature. If not perhaps ever used, the word 'imminent' often hung in the air.

A personal incident can hopefully add some more flavour.

One match day, Yogi had opened the innings, and very unusually had not been the first man out. This was because he had run out his unlucky opening partner Donald Track. I was the next batsmen in. As I made my way from the clubhouse to the wicket, Moira was sitting quietly next to the pitch. Deprived of her usual communications vehicle, who was batting, she called me back, and in her slow and quiet voice whispered:

'Tommy, can you tell Graeme that I've gone.'

Moira had clearly not 'gone' anywhere in terms of leaving, but the gesture she made towards the middle section of her body suggested a more internal situation.

Now, as you walk out to bat in cricket, trying to ensure you get some focus on the challenge ahead is key to early survival. There is a lot to think about. But sadly, it was impossible to move beyond the how and why of Moira having 'gone'. The image was unpleasant but unshakeable in my brain. I duly delivered my message to a largely uninterested Yogi. I did not have a good day batting. For the uninitiated, the shortest possible individual innings lasts one ball. I shall say no more.

In this context, Yogi's 'bittersweet' announcement was made. It suggested that this marriage was to be one of these heart-breaking death bed commitments, tragic in reality and loved by the tabloids.

By this point in the chapter you may be thinking, 'What an utter bastard this writer is, trying to find humour in such circumstances.' In the absence of OG legal expert Trevor Stone, I will self-defend.

In all the years I knew Moira she drank consistently, curried furiously, and had a continuous series of foreign holidays. She never missed a day from her job as a Glasgow traffic warden, and she cycled 12 miles daily to and from her depot. She was, moreover, always first by sprinting to the mid-innings buffet.

I had my doubts at the time, and a much more recent conversation 30 years on with former OGs batsman and fitness addict Keith Lochkin confirmed these.

'Looking good, Keith, clearly keeping in shape.'

'I try my best,' he modestly replied.

'Anything in particular?'

'Well, I did the Glasgow half marathon last Sunday.'

'And by the way, who do you think sprinted past me to the finish line? None other than Moira Kilbride!'

Clearly, what had 'gone' all those years ago as I walked out to bat, had returned. In conclusion, I believe my suspicions on the true nature of Moira's health are justified.

But back to that long ago summer as Yogi and Moira's nuptials beckoned.

A strange precursor to the happy day took place at an evening match the week before. Harry Jamieson, our jovial, happy-go-lucky Brummie wicketkeeper, looked surprisingly concerned in the dressing room after the game. 'Gloves', as he was known (no idea why), eventually said to the four or five people left:

'Yogi's asked me to be his best man.'

'Great, didn't realise you and him were that friendly,' I replied.

'Well that's the thing. As you know, I only joined the OGs in the middle of last season; I barely know him.'

This actually was the basis of Yogi's selection of his right-hand man for the big day: Gloves had fewer years of giving him abuse than any other OG, and less knowledge of past misdemeanours that may have slipped into a speech.

'You'll be fine. Just look supportive, in control, and say a few meaningless words,' soothed Ritchie Cameron, a long standing OG who, with the honing of these skills, went on to a long and distinguished career as a Procurator Fiscal.

'It's not that; I don't mind that sort of thing,' said Gloves.

'So what's the problem?' Ritchie continued.

'Well,' said Gloves, 'it's a bit embarrassing, but do you not think for the best man's speech I should know Yogi's actual name?'

After a bit of reflection, some of the older hands remembered 'Graeme Kilbride'. Relieved, Gloves left feeling a lot more confident about his role in the big day.

Day 1 – the wedding

Ever a loyal and quality act, Yogi chose the OG clubhouse for the wedding reception. This could not have been a selection based on an in-depth analysis of the many fine wedding venues in west central Scotland. Evan Tron suggested this was because Yogi had exhausted these in previous marriages, and that an ill-informed member of staff may have reported him for bigamy mid-celebrations.

The best that could be said of the clubhouse was that it had 'character' – but sadly in this case, the character of a complete shithole. Cheaply built from breeze block, and lacking any flooring, it had never actually been completed due to cash flow issues.[66] The toilets were shared between bar and dressing

---

[66] New to the club at the time, Denzil volunteered to manage the construction budget at a critical phase. Having agreed to this, Paisley Rugby Club were too embarrassed to legally pursue the sums owing.

rooms, and not perhaps subject to the most rigorous cleaning schedule. Slapping a temporary 'Women' sign on one cubicle for the big day did not even pass the lax equal opportunities regime of the 1980s.

But three key features balanced these potential weaknesses: a pool table; a dart board; and very cheap drink. All of these were to play their part as the evening progressed.

It was a smaller gathering than anticipated. Yogi's initial announcement that the OGs were all invited transpired to mean that the OGs were pretty much the only people invited. Only Moira's English parents and Yogi's dad Enoch Kilbride swelled our ranks. And, of course, Bounty.

The early stages were reasonably normal. Gloves gave a surprisingly good speech, though perhaps he overdid the importance of his 17 run partnership with Yogi in a rain-affected bounce match in May.[67] To those in the know, a close post-reading of the speech text would highlight this as the only actual anecdote.

---

[67] Not a significant cricketing achievement likely to forge a strong bond.

And as ever, Denzil unhelpfully contributed by shouting out, after Gloves congratulated the happy couple Graeme and Moira, 'Who the fuck's Graeme?'

Gloves ended his speech by inviting the groom to step up and say a few words. Unknown to us all, Tron then released a backdrop banner: 'Best wishes from all at Yellowstone Park'. It went down very well with the audience, with the exception of the groom and the bride's increasingly uncomfortable-looking parents.

To be fair, Yogi's speech was going quite well until an unfortunate incident. In the small bar space, the pool table dominated the middle of the room. Yogi and Gloves had to speak across this to the accumulated crowd on the other side. This was not ideal, but manageable – as long as no-one was playing pool.

I now need to digress to provide a further detail that becomes central to our story. The clubhouse was in fact the home of Paisley Rugby Club. The cricket club were only tenants, allowed to use it in the rugby closed season months. This relationship was becoming increasingly fractious as the rugby season expanded into both ends of the summer. As a consequence, the rugby team were now viewing the cricket as a growing inconvenience, a situation that ultimately demanded our decampment to Kilmacolm.

Yogi's wedding reception unfortunately coincided with the first night of rugby pre-season training. As the rugby players arrived, they anticipated a good initial workout followed by a quiet pint. The sight of the bar packed with the cricket team did not go down well. A stand had to be made.

Initially all was calm, the rugby training took place outside and did not impact on our party. But Yogi was not a lucky man, and his speech had only begun when the planned rugby protest got underway in earnest. Between Yogi and his audience marched four large and sweaty rugby players still in their training kit. They popped 20 pence into the machine and proceeded to rack up the pool balls.

Yogi had all but physically disappeared from his audience, and the sound of the clacking balls was not helping the acoustics.

Ever the man for a crisis, diplomatic Trevor Stone approached the rugby guys.

'Look, I know this is not ideal, but we did book the club for a wedding reception tonight. Would you mind if we could just get this bit over with?'

The rugby players looked sympathetic. 'OK, who did you book it with?'

All eyes looked to Yogi. 'Eh, the Building Convenor.'

'Funny that,' replied the prop forward about to take his shot, 'I'm the Building Convenor.'

Sheepishly, Yogi continued. 'Well, I didn't book it as such, you know it's the cricket season, didn't think you guys would be about...'

'So it's not booked,' came the unanswerable response.

'No.'

This was tense, but again we were indebted to Trevor Stone. He quietly took the Building Convenor aside, and after a few moments of amicable conversation, returned. He whispered in Yogi's ear, and then announced:

'The rugby guys have been reasonable; Yogi will be allowed to complete his speech before they recommence their pool game. Thereafter, they are all invited to join the wedding, including free drinks.'

'One condition,' shouted Jamie Grip. 'Can they get showered and changed first?'

Trevor Stone looked at the rugby players, and after a short consultative huddle, a thumbs-up was communicated with the proviso, 'Once we've completed this game.'

'OK Yogi,' said Trevor, 'finish your speech *exactly* as we agreed.'

Yogi cleared his throat. 'Thank you for coming.'

True to their word, our rugby colleagues showered and then partied as hard as any of us for the rest of the night. It was never clear whether Trevor had meant to extend the free drink invitation to the other eight guys in the changing room, but they 'took one for the team' and fully participated in the evening's festivities. They seemed to thoroughly enjoy themselves, and all managed to deal adequately with Frank Uber's inevitable approach as to whether they had ever considered cricket.

Following the abrupt termination of Yogi's speech, his earlier decision to cut reception costs then led to a less than successful musical interlude.

'Between' major ventures, Denzil had teamed up with fellow OG Dawid Biro to form a semi-professional two-man group, The Entrepreneurs. Astonishingly, Yogi hired them for the night, having negotiated down to a joint performance fee of £5.

'Good evening Paisley!' shouted Denzil, making a sort of black power fist to the sceptical crowd.

'We'd like to open up with a stripped back reggae twist on an old classic.'

Beating his guitar rhythmically if not tunefully, Bob Marley did not come to mind. Denzil let rip:

> *'Plea-ea-ease release me let me go-o-o-o-o;*
> *For I-I-I don't love you anymo-o-o-ore;*
> *To li-i-i-ive a lie would be a si-i-i-i-in;*
> *Release me and let me love agai-ai-ai-ain.'*

The crowd stood frozen. Even with Yogi's track record, this song about the collapse of a relationship seemed inappropriate at his wedding reception.

The Entrepreneurs carried on, interpreting the glazed looks of the audience as indicative of awe at their musical genius.

'I-I-I have found a new love dea-ea-ea-ear;
'And she will always want me nea-ea-ea-ear.'

'Enough!' Trevor Stone interjected by grabbing the microphone. 'Many thanks, to Denzil and Dawid for a spirited effort.'

'I will pop out to my car and get a cassette of some early unpublished Bach variations which may be a more appropriate musical backdrop to the evening's celebrations.' Trevor genuinely seemed to think this would help.

Denzil seemed surprised but, as ever, not broken. Dawid, who to this point had not appeared to do anything other than jiggle in a way that suggested less of a Caribbean vibe than the need to go to the toilet, put away his as yet unused mouth organ.

Denzil being Denzil saw the positives. Later in the evening he approached me.

'Thought it went pretty well, all in all. Just maybe the wrong audience. It can happen, I guess, when you are musically innovating. Dawid and I want to create a lasting musical legacy, not just make easy cash. Anyone can do that sort of lightweight Abba stuff.'

I did not respond.

'It's just a pity we didn't manage to squeeze in our second song - a truly emotional *a cappella* version of Carole King's *It's Too Late*. Without the distraction of instruments, you can really absorb the full impact of the lyrics. I was going to ask Yogi and Moira to take to the floor for the first dance of the evening at this point.'

For those unfamiliar, this song is a moving reflection on a dying relationship, containing such painful lines as, 'Something inside has died, I can't hide it, and I just can't fake it.' In the right context it is a wonderful song, but not one to open the batting at a wedding. It also later transpired that Denzil had actually planned to end his set with a disco version of Neil Diamond's *Love on the Rocks*. A lack of contextual awareness was one of his many shortfalls.

Despite these initial setbacks, in the end it was a good night, soured only slightly by a couple of further incidents.

As the evening progressed, Archie Ranger teamed up with the man 50% responsible for Yogi, his father Enoch Kilbride. A cantankerous widower in his late 60s, he harboured some extreme right-wing views, alongside a love of good malt whisky.

He was an old associate of Archie, and they fell into the two pastimes for which Scotland could win international awards: excessive drinking and talking shite. The conversation was also characterised by two other very Scottish things – extreme loudness, and a misleading impression that they were involved in a hostile argument. Far from it; both friends were having a great time.

Enoch was no doubt a loving and supportive father, but this did not debar him from having a strong objective sense of his son's failings. For example, I was introduced to him at the bar earlier in the evening.

'Tommy, yes Yogi has mentioned you play with him.'

Filled with a sense of wellbeing towards Yogi on his wedding night, and not entirely sober, I replied,

'Yes, pretty solid player.'

Enoch paused, looked at me quizzically, and delivered a damningly accurate reply.

'The problem with Graeme [real name used so obviously signalling a criticism], is that he has never been anything like as good at cricket as he thinks he is.'

Enoch roared with laughter.

It was difficult to argue with the accuracy of the observation. But it was, I felt, a tad unnecessary on his son's big night. It was also delivered at a volume deliberately pitched to maximise the audience. This included Moira's parents, who by now were thinking their decision to come up from Oldham for the weekend was a mistake.

But worse was to come.

As mentioned, Yogi was not tying the knot for the first time. Many frogs had been tongued until he found his Princess in Moira. But just how many?

All other conversation gradually came to halt as Archie bellowed:

'Sorry Enoch – wrong. Definitely five, not counting Moira.'

'Archie, I'm his dad for Christ's sake, I'd know. Maximum four.'

'Right, let's count!'

It was then that the final piece of clubhouse equipment came to the fore – the dart board; or more accurately, its accompanying scoring blackboard.

'Jim Track, you can probably count as well as anyone, write it up,' instructed Archie.

Jim duly grabbed a piece of chalk.

'Write, Jim. One: young Irene, his school sweetheart,' Archie announced.

'Agreed,' acknowledged Enoch.

'Two: big Linda, the barmaid from the Bull Inn.'

'A very bad mistake,' admitted Enoch.

'Three: Jean, his aunt, but by marriage.'

Enoch was beginning to look worried. 'But to be fair, Archie, that was a very short-term consoling gesture when his Uncle Tam died so suddenly, leaving her bereft.'

'Still counts!' Archie was on a roll and commanding the room.

'Four: the lassie from Tonga who came down to Dumfries with us.'

'But you know that was only a visa-related thing. Indicative of Yogi's kind heart.'

'A marriage is a marriage. Write it up, Jim.'

'Now you're stuck,' Enoch fought back.

Jim paused, but only for effect.

'Number five: Sarah Lou, the country and western singer that he met in Govan's Grand Ole Opry.'

People in the know fell silent. It had been widely rumoured that Enoch himself, mesmerised by Sarah Lou's quirky Cajun/bluegrass fusion, had also had a dalliance with the six-foot Texan. It was a source of some tension between father and son. Yogi had never been able to bring himself to admit his subsequent five-week marriage.

For a few seconds, Enoch looked crestfallen. Archie had triumphed, though the context of winning and losing seemed to pall into insignificance, given that this had been played out publicly at his son's (as we had now established) sixth wedding reception.

Moira's parents looked older and very tired. It was no surprise when they shortly thereafter said it had been a 'memorable' night, but now they had best get back to their hotel.

Enoch was not a man to hold grudges. Archie's offer of 'quits and a double malt' was accepted and all was forgiven.

The night moved to its inevitably hazy ending. Yogi, rattled by earlier events, upped his alcohol intake even further, eventually joining Archie and Enoch at the bar for a furious last half hour of drinking. It was a truly touching moment of father and son bonding.

Eventually the taxi arrived to whisk the newlyweds back to their hotel for a night of unbridled passion. But when the taxi arrived, the driver took one look at the state of the groom and with some justification said, 'There's no way he's getting in my cab.'

But he had not realised that his long-time nemesis Frank Uber was a wedding guest.

'Majid!' he cried. 'We meet again. Have you finally decided to accept my offer and join up? I could show you around for a minute.'

Majid froze. 'Just get him in the car – now.' He gestured to best man Gloves. It was over in a second: Moira shoved Yogi in and followed.

And the happy couple's taxi light dimmed into the Paisley night as they set off on their new life together. But Yogi's condition, and the coolness of Moira post the dart board incident, suggested their night of passion and formal marriage consummation may have been put back a bit.

Day 2 – worse

Yogi's wedding had not best prepared our squad for a tricky away tie the next day. This was against the factory team of Rolls Royce in the nearby town of East Kilbride.

Returning to T.S. Eliot – who styled his name from cricket score books: 'Summer surprised us.' The day awoke bright and sunny, and across Scotland scores of fresh early risers were ready to seize what may be one of the last good days of the year. Not the OGs. As the starting time of 1pm approached, a dishevelled set of creatures slowly amassed at the ground. The Rolls Royce boys looking on did not seem overly impressed.

'Christ, look at this mob. Get them batting first and I might get to my mid-afternoon BBQ after all,' one commented a little too loudly.

'OK,' captain Donald Track said, 'I count ten, who are we missing?'

'Yogi,' piped up Trevor Stone.

Given the night before, this did not surprise anyone. And frankly, would he be missed? But just at that moment, a taxi rounded the corner. Unbelievably, out popped Yogi, his new bride, and his new in-laws.

On reflection, Yogi appearing did not surprise. After the previous night I could imagine Moira saying, when he asked about the cricket, 'Just go! Go fucken anywhere!'

But fair play to her; as a portent of what became many years of loyalty, she was there standing shoulder to shoulder with her cricketing warrior. As to why Moira's parents turned up, we can only speculate. One theory was that despite all, Yogi had managed to convince them that watching him perform at cricket was well worth an extended stay in Scotland. But Evan Tron probably nailed it more accurately with the simple observation, 'Have you ever been to Oldham?'

We lost the toss and were asked to bat first by the BBQ-eyeing Rolls Royce skipper.

'Yogi, you go in first and try and recover your already shaky marriage by impressing your new in-laws,' instructed mischievous skipper Donald Track. 'Tommy, shit as you look, others seem worse. You go in at three after the first wicket.'

This is important detail, as is my need to briefly digress on the nature of the playing infrastructure.

In most sports it is common for the viewing area to look out on to where the action is happening. Football stands, for example, face the pitch; Wimbledon stands face the court. And so on. This would seem obvious. Not, alas, to whoever constructed Rolls Royce's cricket pitch.

For some reason, the clubhouse and playing area appeared to have at best a distant relationship to each other; say, a sort of third cousin. Looking directly out from the clubhouse, the cricket pitch was over your left shoulder just beyond the 90-degree point. It was a unique set up, and about as badly designed as imaginable.

This was unfortunate in terms of viewing low grade Scottish club cricket. But for me, it has always had much more serious implications. Rolls Royce, as you will likely know, is a worldwide brand famous for precision engineering. This was the ground of their works team from the then (but sadly no longer) prestigious Scottish base. With all the design brains in that place, how hard could it have been to work out that a viewing area required to enable viewing?

As a result, since my first experience of playing at Rolls Royce, I have been a nervous flier. Rolls Royce engines are hugely popular on many types of airplanes. As I look out of a plane window, I often wonder if the engines were made by the same guy who designed the cricket pitch. I am not comforted.

To counterbalance this entirely unjustified dig at Rolls Royce East Kilbride, I think it is only fair to reference the factory's greatest moment. This was in the 1970s, when the workers at the plant boycotted servicing the Hawker Hunter jet planes used by Chilean fascist dictator General Pinochet to oust the democratically elected regime of Salvador Allende. It was a superb act of international solidarity, retold 40 years later in the fine documentary 'Nae Pasaran'.[68] With all due respect, it somewhat outranked any achievements of the factory's cricket team.

Back to the game. As we sat looking over our left shoulders, Yogi and his fellow opener Donald Track strode to the wicket to start the game.

'Go on, love, show them what you can do,' were Moira's kind parting words to Yogi.

This was exactly what we were worried about. In a way it reminded me of the sweethearts from 1914 waving off their husbands from Victoria Station to the western front. Trying desperately to stay hopeful but fearing the worst.

A few overs passed uneventfully, though without being actually being able to see, this was mainly guesswork.

---

[68] It should for historical balance be noted that Pinochet was not without friends. A great admirer was Margaret Thatcher, who offered the dictator asylum in the UK when he was rumbled by the Chileans, and sent her 'old friend' malt whisky when he was finally placed under house arrest by the incoming 1997 Labour Government. Thatcher was clearly after the period when Britain was good at fighting fascists. Also, Allende was a bit of leftie: this democracy lark has its limits.

Then up went the cry: 'Yogi's out!'

This fell into the inevitable rather than surprising category.

But then another cry, from young aspiring, but hopeless and desperately small, Greg Omelette (forever hereafter known as 'Tonto'), who had been posted up field to scout and relay messages back to base camp.

Next in, I sprung to my feet.

'Maybe not. He's stopped,' Tonto shouted again.

'How was he out?'

'No idea,' replied Tonto. 'Couldn't see anything. Certainly not bowled; the bowling team seem more entertained than celebrating.'

I had no idea whether to head up country or not.

'He's definitely coming off,' Tonto updated.

I headed out. Yogi was walking towards me with a very slow and uncertain shuffle. Something like an uncoordinated death march. Finally, I reached him.

'What's happening, how were you out?' I asked. Without looking at me, he raised a limp hand and moved on.

I looked back, and suddenly three senses were engaged at once. A large brown stain, an unpleasant squelching sound, and a horrendous smell.

By now, I suspect you have solved the riddle. Yogi was not 'out' in cricketing terms; stretching for a wide ball, he had monumentally shat himself. The last half hour of furious drinking with his dad and Archie the night before, and an undercooked chicken vol-au-vent, had hit back big style.

As I reached the middle, I was again conscious of not being mentally focused on the batting challenge ahead. But this time it was of no consequence. The Rolls Royce players, many visibly crying with laughter, were even less well prepared. The normal quick confab with the other remaining batsman also failed. Donald Track took a few steps forward, looked at me, and stumbled to the ground.

A full five minutes elapsed before we could try and return to cricket. A few times the bowler broke down in his run up, and twice I had to step back because of uncontrolled sniggering in the slip cordon. To be fair, my update that it was the day after his wedding night and that his wife and new in-laws were watching, was not, on balance, helpful to any restart aspirations.

How the game finished, I cannot remember. But what I can recall was my frustration as I stood in the middle batting, aware I was missing a dressing room scene of truly epic dimensions.

When I did return, Moira and Yogi's new in-laws had departed, and Yogi sat squeezed into an extra pair of trousers supplied by 15-year-old Tonto. The embers of a small fire were pointed out some 20 yards from the clubhouse: the remains of Yogi's previous outfit.

One suspects that the formal consummation of the marriage was again delayed.

Chapter 11 – A Scottish Sporting Story

'That fought and died for, your wee bit hill and glen'.

'Flower of Scotland' – The Corries

Jack 'Red Can' Donald was an OG from my early days with the club and would feature more in these memoirs if he had not headed down south with work in his mid-20s.

He was a fine cricketer – a naturally gifted wicket keeper and dedicated if unspectacular batsmen.

In our younger years, Jack and I represented Scotland's under-16s together. Though playing for different clubs at the time, we knew each other from school and were natural roommates on away trips – particularly as we were the only people in the team not from east of Scotland public schools.

Playing at this level meant Jack would easily make an important cricketing contribution to the OGs. But on a trip to Leeds to play a Yorkshire Colts team, he truly established his early credentials to become an all-time OG legend.

Jack had one huge advantage at this point: I was 15 and looked about 12, Jack was 15 and looked to be in his mid-30s. This mattered. Not only could he cop off with divorced and sexually experienced women, but he was also a guaranteed supplier of under-age drink. At a certain age in Scotland, such people assume an almost regal status.

After day one of our game against the Yorkshire Colts, we were in a surprisingly competitive position. (Normally English cricket sides were much too strong for their Scottish counterparts.) It was all very serious – actual coaches giving post-match analysis, technical tips, and motivational talks. For the first time I discovered the strange concept of 'tactics'.

Released back to our lodgings in an old-style university hall of residence, Jack immediately announced, 'Right, quick change and out. We're meeting some of the other guys downstairs in 15 minutes.'

'But we've had our tea, and I don't fancy the pictures,' I naively replied.

'Are you daft?' Jack looked at me in genuine amazement. 'We are going to get pissed!'

'I'll not get served.'

'Don't worry,' he replied. 'Apparently they don't give a shit about under-age drinking down here. We'll find a big pub, I'll get them in, and the rest of you can sit in a corner somewhere.'

Incredibly, it worked. A night of heavy drinking ensured, though in my youthful state, this involved being unable to finish a second pint of Tetley bitter. Not so Jack, a much more experienced drinker who had started as soon as he looked 18. This had meant by the time of this story, he had approaching six years of resilience in the tank. Frustrated at the pathetic pace of his drinking companions, Jack moved swiftly on to shorts, and disgusted at the 'mean English measures', quickly moved through the gears from doubles to trebles.

Eventually, persuading him that progressing to a brothel was not a great idea, with some help I got him back to our digs. Being physically quite a bit bigger than the rest of us, this was quite a feat. Exhausted, once we got him in the building, he was left in the wide halls of residence corridor, already asleep.

Job done, I headed to our room, anticipating a peaceful night on my own. But then coming up the stairs, I heard super-enthusiastic head coach Davie Thomson calling, 'Just checking you guys are all in for a good night's sleep.' He was heading for where Jack lay. To be fair, Jack was asleep, but young as I was, I worked out this was not quite what Davie was getting at.

I hared down the corridor towards a now snoring heavily and contented looking Jack. On my own, I could not possibly lift him, and he could not be awoken.

To this day, Jack has no idea how much he owes to the beautifully polished old school wooden floors in the halls of residence corridors. Turning him on his back, I grabbed his two arms and slid him back to our room just in time.

Lying on my bed exhausted, Davie shouted through the door:

'You two OK in there?'

'Yes, fine thanks,' I replied.

'And Jack?'

'Yes. Sound asleep already. No pre-match day nerves for him.'

My lifetime as a fairly convincing liar may date from this point.

Needless to say, in classic Scottish sporting tradition, our significantly hungover side subsided to a crushing defeat on day two.

'Hard to explain,' a deflated coach and scout master Davie Thomson reflected on the coach back north. 'The vagaries of the sport, but in a way reflective of the magic of the game.'

All heads turned accusingly to Jack. But he was again happily asleep, still recovering from the night before.

I have one final reflection on this tale. Jack 'Red Can' Donald has never properly thanked me for my rescue act that night, mainly because for many years he has simply refused to accept it ever happened. If you are reading Jack, you still owe me!

Chapter 12 – Do you do naan bread?[69]

'There are three things, and three things only that can lift the pain of mortality and ease the ravages of life,' said Spider. 'These things are wine, women and song.'

'Curry's nice too,' pointed out fat Charlie.

Neil Gaiman – Anansi Boys

Curry is a major feature of Scottish sport, and in the Glasgow area we are truly spoiled by what is one of the best concentrations of curry houses in Europe. So important are curries, that some of the guys who own the restaurants have become local celebrities. Hats off to them and well deserved; they have truly contributed to the common weal.

---

[69] This book was mainly written before a major racism scandal hit Scottish cricket in 2022. This is not a place to comment in any detail on this, other than to note the controversial findings made for uncomfortable reading. Hopefully it will trigger some long overdue change. Cricket should be one of the last sports for racism; any lover of the game is brought up worshipping so many all-time greats of the game who were people of colour. How this then transmutes into the superiority inherent in racism is beyond me.

In victory or defeat, curry is a balm. Not only the food, but the whole ambience of a good curry house. This is true the world over. But it is a perhaps a more Scottish male twist or misunderstanding that, after participating in sport, you are legally debarred from entering an Indian restaurant unless you have consumed a minimum of six pints of beer.

Curiously, I have a theory that – properly communicated – this may help us finally rid Scotland of racism.

Self-evidently, racism is an awful thing. As a white person, I can see this clearly; God knows what it must be like to experience it. So much of it is difficult to understand, and amongst the far too many racists still out there, one thing always puzzles me: a complete lack of self-awareness. You repeatedly open your mouth as a blowhard pub bore or know-it-all taxi driver, and are unaware you could just short cut this by wearing a big badge, 'I am an uncool, idiot cunt.'[70] It would save energy and time.

---

[70] This is the only use of the 'C' word in these tales, as it seems, as Flaubert, would concur, *le mot juste*. But in many ways, this is unfortunate. As very well-articulated in Kate Lister's 'A Curious History of Sex', the 'C' word has had a very bad press. It should arguably be a feminist word, and historically had much more acceptable usage. There are some anatomical reasons for this. I would strongly recommend Kate Lister's book – informative and very, very funny.

Underpinning racism is a sense of superiority: we are better than you. We apply this to countries, religions, sexuality, skin colours, gender. Generalising in this way is always wrong, and it is lazy by allowing us not to think.

Rant over. I will get back to my theory of drink and curries.

I think the Scottish Government, who already do some good stuff tackling this, should commission a behavioural change agency to establish a hidden camera in, say, six Glasgow Indian or Pakistani restaurants between 11pm and 1am on Friday and Saturday nights. It would not take long until a polite, hard-working and helpful group of waiters welcomed a drunken marauding horde of sports-playing natives.

The drama would play out, sometimes good humoured, sometimes not. Sadly, there is too often one idiot who will shout some unfunny and desperately obvious racist 'joke'. (You know the guy – the one that's not racist, and generally not very nice.)

A vat of beer is immediately summoned, but then it gets difficult: ordering food.

Even the simplest menu is beyond the group.

'Is this hot?' – fair.

'Can I have chips with this?' – idiotic.

'Can I have the same as I had the last time?' – unhelpful, because it is the first time they have ever been in the restaurant.

'Can I have the biryani, leaving out the curry?' – nonsensical.

'Whereabouts in India is the Chicken Maryland from?' – no words.

'Hey Abdul, can you give me this menu in English?' – the non-racist funny guy.

A polite, non-drinking waiter patiently observes and tries to make sense of this. Trying to be helpful and deflecting abuse, he finally manages to interpret some form of meal order.

More beer, the food arrives, and further chaos ensues. There is commonly one major cause of this: after 5-10 minutes, no-one has the slightest idea what they ordered.

Eventually the waiter – now often with a back-up colleague – has to take control. He distributes the food as best he can remember, probably conscious by this time that it doesn't really matter.

The scene of actually eating the food is best passed over. It is not pretty and can sometimes only be rectified by an industrial cleaning company.

And then the final denouement: the bill. This commonly makes the ordering of the food look like a straightforward exercise. The waiter will normally target the person who appears most sober; in this quest he normally has very few, if any, options.

The waiter is also aware at this point that the original 10 diners has reduced to seven, and another is sound asleep in the remnants of their otherwise untouched Mango Halwa. Two are understood to be in the toilets, another is reported as 'missing in action'.

It takes some time. The suggestion that people pay individually is quickly dismissed, and the instruction on the menu that groups over six cannot do this is politely pointed out. There then follows another excruciating moment when it is suggested they all divvy up based on what they actually ate. But this hits three key stumbling blocks: no-one can remember what they ordered; three of the diners are not actually present; and another is asleep.

I have no idea how the bill is actually paid in these circumstances. My only guess is that someone marginally more sober pays up a negotiated amount. This is likely to be assisted if at least one person in the group has a job where an arrest in a curry house may adversely affect future promotion prospects.

With stray colleagues awakened and retrieved from the toilets, the group staggers out into the night for more drink.

Similar scenes have been captured on Scottish Government cameras across Glasgow. The challenge now is to turn the edited highlights into an anti-racism campaign and add a short caption:

'This clip shows the interaction of two racial groups – white Scotsmen and Indian waiting staff.

'In the morning, some people in one of the groups will think they are racially and culturally superior.

'You decide.'[71]

The OGs were undoubtedly guilty of many of these behaviours, but hopefully not the more

---

[71] I'd like to think in Scotland we are improving on these issues, but we have a way to go.

unpleasant aspects. In this, we were perhaps fortunate to have in our ranks Faheed and Wasim, two Scottish Pakistani cousins who ran a good curry shop in Paisley, The Lahore.

How this knowledge was originally introduced provides me with an opportunity to briefly 'honour' another OG eccentric.

In an early season game, we batted first. This then provides the nine guys not actually at the wicket endless time to talk whilst looking on. As anyone who has ever played cricket would concur, this is an opportunity to generate more utterly inane conversation than in almost any other human endeavour. Because of the amount of time available, and the idea we are notionally watching the cricket, these are very odd conversations. There can often be a minute or more between statement and response. There is simply no hurry.

Into this arena steps OG middle order bat, Stephen Carew, a humourless, grey man, who took his cricket very seriously. Over time he built a reputation for making extraordinarily obvious statements. Normally these tended to be laced with pessimism, for example:

'Do you think that big fast bowler will be trying to get me out?'

'Do you think that massive, dark cloud coming our way means it might rain?'

'Do you think that young group of guys over there with a dozen bottles of Buckfast might get drunk?'

Faheed had just joined the club and sat padded up in the clubhouse. As I was the only OG that previously knew him, I asked:

'Good to see you again, Faheed. What are you up to these days?'

'I've set up a curry restaurant in the centre of town. Going well. You guys should come in some time.'

As was not uncommon, we watched the cricket in silence for a bit. An extended period, with the potential to enable a thoughtful reply. But Stephen spoke first:

'Do you do naan bread?' he queried.

Faheed looked at him puzzled. 'Well, yes.'

Now, I suspect if you even dislike or have never had a curry, you would recognise this as the most unnecessary question imaginable. It would seem be the equivalent of walking into a pub and asking if they sold beer, going to a railway station and checking if it had any trains, or asking a super-rich Tory donor if they avoided tax.

Inane, pointless, but asked with deadly seriousness. A classic Stephen Carew moment.

Stephen moved on to another club soon after this conversation, claiming the OGs' overall approach to the game was too flippant. He had exhausted his conversational repertoire. To be fair, he then became a much better player.

For the record, at that time The Lahore did four varieties of very tasty naan bread.

Over the years, Faheed and Wasim became fine OGs. Physically, they could not have been more different. Faheed, the elder, was a shortish, rotund figure with the build of Santa Claus. Wasim was tall and handsome, with almost film star looks. He reminded me of a Pakistani Seve Ballesteros. I knew Faheed better, having played together as youngsters at a previous club. He was the better cricketer of the cousins – a fine and technically gifted batsman, who scored quickly and was good to watch.

Faheed and Wasim's cousin Haris played for the OGs occasionally as a very young boy, when we were short on numbers. Even then you could see he had inherited Faheed's skills, and then some. He quickly moved on from the OGs and progressed through the levels to become a long standing and very successful Scottish international. He was the only OG to ever to win full international honours. Whether he has ever viewed it in this way is open to question.

Faheed was a true 'cameo' king (see chapter 15). But the reason he became so adept at cameos was different from other players. If batting second, Faheed was always keen to go in early in the batting order and attack from ball one. Building an innings was not his thing. After a few lusty blows he would overreach himself and get out. Most batsmen would be disappointed at this point, but Faheed would walk-off happy, smiling and relaxed.

Once you are out batting in the second innings of a cricket match, your game is over; you cannot contribute further in any way. On that basis, if necessary, you can leave.[72] A common reason for this

---

[72] This may seem a bit harsh – not staying to the last. But over the years, I have seen St. Mirren players – most recently under the management of Alain

would be if you had a special night out planned, or a wedding reception to attend. Faheed had The Lahore, in which he rightly took great pride. After dismissal, he would quickly shower and be off, ready to take charge for another busy Saturday night. To this day, Faheed would probably deny his aggressive shot selection was based on his commitment to the cause of good curries – but we knew!

On a normal home match-day Saturday, that was not the last we saw of Faheed. In the clubhouse, at a late point in the evening, and having suitably replaced the fluids lost in action, the cry would go up from somewhere: 'Lahore!'

On most nights, this would include a core of the predictable OGs, and representatives of our opponents. This camaraderie is a great thing about club cricket, that almost always trumped even the most bitter on-field spats.

One exception was when playing Renfrew. This historically was reported as because, bizarrely, no-one in any Renfrew team ever liked curry. A retrospective discussion on this at a subsequent OGs' reunion, however, subtlety amended the official

---

Nobbes - end their contribution after about 15 minutes of the game, but annoyingly stay on the park for the duration.

record: no-one in the Renfrew team 'had ever been asked if they liked curry'.

But most nights in The Lahore, we had company from our earlier on-field foes. Inevitably, this tended to be the more Rabelaisian of their cohort – loud and drunk. It normally included the primary object of Archie Ranger's earlier abuse, who by this point in the night was giving it back both barrels. Archie loved it.

But after a few unfortunate evenings, reflective of some of the stereotypical behaviour now anticipated to be used in a future Scottish Government campaign, Faheed required to make a stand.

Another characteristic shared by Faheed and Wasim was their most outstanding broad smile. This reflected their overall charm and purposeful patience. A smile from either could simultaneously communicate friendliness, admonition and sympathy. It was like getting a mild reprimand from your favourite uncle. This attribute was employed by Faheed after a particularly difficult night in The Lahore.

'It was great to see you all again on Saturday. But some of the staff felt a bit angered at your behaviour. My young cousin Asif is just over from Islamabad to get some experience. He says it took him a full 20 minutes to get just the starter order. You owe me £24, and you left Red Can unconscious in the toilet.'

We all looked down sheepishly. Factually, it was a damningly accurate assessment, with Asif possibly going a bit easy on the starter order. My memory was that this took nearer half-an-hour.

'Now, I don't want to bar you, but things have got to change. Wasim and I have had a chat and we propose future access arrangements on the following basis.'

Wasim then passed copies of a short note around the dressing room.

No more than 10 in one group.

Fixed two course menu of our [Lahore staff's] choosing – i.e. no ordering.

Fixed cost of £10 per head.

Full payment in advance, and prior to the supply of any alcohol.

Nominated lead diner, responsible for ensuring all of the party leave the premises when requested (including toilet checks).

All of the above is not for negotiation.

'We will now leave the room to enable discussion,' Wasim beamed. 'We will return in five minutes for your decision.'

After a very brief discussion, we realised our negotiating position was not strong. The Lahore knocked out a fine curry, and frankly where else would have us. We appeared to hold about as many cards as a Tory toff trying to negotiate a post-Brexit trade deal.

Faheed and Wasim returned in exactly five minutes.

'Deal!' announced nominated spokesman Trevor Stone.

Faheed and Wasim's smiles returned broader than ever. It proved a successful and lasting arrangement, which seemed to work well for both sides. The phrase 'ten tenners' worth' passed into OGs legend.

The new Lahore regime was well established by the year Jack 'Red Can' Donald took over the club captaincy. It is Jack more than anyone I remember currying with at this time, and who was responsible for the concept of the 'counselling curry'. Hard as it is to believe, this story is from Jack's more mature and sensible years. A snapshot into his younger life is given in chapter 11.

Red Can was named after a famous Scottish beer to which he quite was partial. It is still available today, and in my opinion stands comparison with many fine new pale ales, and knocks real ale into a cocked hat.

Jack was a strange combination in many ways. Though a true 'lover of life', he was a good player who took his cricket seriously. At a young age he was made club captain, and unlike the usually conscript nature of this position, Jack saw it as an opportunity to lift the OGs to a whole new level. There is really no explanation as to what went wrong. Initially amongst the favourites for promotion, the season went from bad to worse, and before we knew it, we were facing the real prospect of relegation.

Jack took this very badly, and as the side foundered, his personal form disintegrated. He blamed it all on himself, and refused to accept that we had all just been a bit shit.

From an already lofty base, his post-match consumption of Red Cans rocketed further. Two or three normally perished before he showered, and some local shops began to ration his purchases. His night of despair regularly ended in The Lahore. It's fair to say that he was, by this late stage in the evening, not the best of company - very drunk and muttering incoherently in a self-admonishing manner. Often, he just collapsed into his curry.

Again, Faheed had to intervene. Red Can's crime on these occasions was not the usual drunken loudness. Rather, many other diners did not relish a fun Saturday night out sitting near a grown man in such obvious distress.

This came to a head one night late in the season, when a nervous young diner pulled Faheed aside and said his planned romantic proposal of marriage had required to be postponed, because by the crucial moment, his intended fiancée was crying in sympathy with Jack's despair.

'Look,' Faheed said, 'I do feel Jack's pain, and I know I am one of the guys that keeps letting him down. But I've a business to run.

'It's not ideal, but I've a small room through the back we don't use. We could kit it out a bit, and three of you could sit in there, including of course the skipper.'

And so, the 'counselling curry' was born.

Until the end of the season, two teammates were rostered to join Jack in this anteroom. No-one was allowed to tell Jack this was happening. If, drunk as he was, he happened to ask why three of us had to go into an overflow room in a clearly half-empty restaurant, Faheed agreed to say he was awaiting a coach party, which surprisingly never ever arrived.

On a happier note, a lucky combination of weather-ruined games and a stuffy and tense last day victory, meant Jack ultimately steered his hapless crew to league survival. He celebrated by getting exceptionally drunk on Red Cans and falling asleep in his curry. But this time, he was allowed to stay in the main room.

Around a decade later, and long after the OGs had folded, I was walking back from a St. Mirren game early on a lovely spring evening, when I passed on the far side of the street from The Lahore.

For most, it was still too early for curries, and Faheed was standing outside, taking a break from food preparations and enjoying the fine weather. Having moved from Paisley, I hadn't seen him in many years.

He signalled to me, and I waved back. Then he beckoned for me and my two pals to come over.

'Hold on a second,' he said, and went back inside. He quickly returned with a very large bag of mixed pakora. 'On the house.'

'Many thanks!'

It does not take any invitation for a Scotsman to dive in on such an occasion, and the three of us duly did so. 'Outstanding!' we muffled, unable to stop eating.

Faheed then looked me in the eye, ever mischievous, and with his broadest smile said:

'Tommy, you came in here so often late on a Saturday night a bit the worse for wear for your 'tenner's worth'. I thought for just once in your life you deserved some of the good stuff!'

He winked at me and went back into The Lahore.

Chapter 13 – Comrade Sherwood

'And it's higher and higher and higher
With our emblem the Soviet Star
And every propeller is turning
In defence of the USSR.'

Song of the Soviet airmen.

Henry Sherwood is the only known Stalinist to have played for the OGs. Ironically, perhaps, he was a 'blue blood' – a genuine former pupil, and with the best credentials possible, having attended the Grammar primary school from aged five. Over the years, it is fair to say his politics drifted somewhat from the school's mainstream orthodoxy.

If, in later years, Henry had been the first person to split the atom he would not have received an acknowledgement in the 'News of former pupils' section of the *Grammarian* magazine. 'A bloody Commie!' I can hear the editor cry. 'Replace him with that wee guy who's just become a Tory Councillor in Thornly Park, or something about Fred Goodwin's holidays.'[73]

But Henry was a follower, not a leader. The real thinker was his long-term partner Natasha, and it became clear she was the political driver in their relationship – guiding, reinforcing, and, one could argue, terrifying Henry into accepting that Joseph Stalin was the greatest figure in world history.

This is not as strange as it may sound. Natasha was irresistible. We were all secretly infatuated by her: though on one level Henry was a bit pathetic, in many ways he seemed the luckiest man alive. To men of a certain age and time (and I suspect quite a few woman), this was a combo of Helen Mirren meets Joanna Lumley meets Greta Scacchi. Henry was not the only OG hopelessly in love with her. In looks, class, tan, skin and movement, she had it all. It turned out her real name was actually Jean, but this mattered not a jot. She was a better 'Natasha'.

And there was one key thing so easily forgotten when in her company: at the time of these memoirs, Natasha was approaching 60. Henry was 30.

In conversation, she was mesmeric. Neither before nor since has anyone had quite the same impact on me. Her looks and deportment combined with a posh English voice that seemed at times to

---

[73] Thornly Park is a very affluent area of Paisley. Often you cannot see the houses from the street. Winning it for Tories is not a big deal. Enough said.

sing; and at key points she spoke through a smile that could make you weak. It was deeply perplexing, because everything she actually said was total nonsense.

She remained a completely unreconstructed Stalinist, and repeatedly claimed that East Germany in the 1980s had the highest standard of living on earth; apparently, they only built the Berlin Wall in case people slipped out by accident. Never keen to get into detailed debate, she brushed away our concerns on Stalin's murder in the gulags of up to 15 million people as something that was 'necessary'. Given the scale of the offence, this seemed a bit light as an explanation – but Natasha delivered it well. And anyway, we were simply a group of silly boys, continually in a state of 'false consciousness'.[74]

Although serious political debate was largely avoided, myself and my brother – as the indulged OG 'lefties' – once tried to develop some form of 'broad left' alliance in the OG dressing room. Our advances could not have been more strongly rebuffed. For

---

[74] 'False consciousness' is a Marxist term. It means that because of continuous brainwashing by controlling powers and their media, ordinary people are incapable of understanding anything, and are easily manipulated. It actually has a point, but the phrase became hopelessly overused – and in practice is used to label opponents in any argument. In this respect it has become a bit like Trump's 'fake news' - totally meaningless, and a get out for anything. I am so pleased I have found a connection between Karl Marx and the orange balloon 'loser'.

Natasha, the 'reformist' 1945 Labour government was the real enemy. 'Rather than advancing the cause,' she declared, 'they capitulated to capitalism and ended up in total betrayal.' Ouch, I thought, assuming she included the creation of the National Health Service in this analysis.

As a couple, Natasha and Henry appeared inseparable – leading to them being referred to as a single unit: 'Natashen'. But, as the great P.G. Wodehouse would have noted, Henry was 'not the only onion in the stew.' Natasha and Henry were not married, and their private life was complicated and unconventional. They lived together in a loft apartment in Glasgow's Merchant City with Natasha's actual husband, Carlos, an ageing revolutionary exiled from Chile by Pinochet in 1973. It was all very amicable; Henry worshipped Carlos – although he never appeared at the OGs, despite Frank Uber's best efforts. The sexual permutations were never explained, despite repeated adolescent questioning by teammates.

Whatever your views of Natashen's politics, you could not deny they were the full, dedicated package. For Natasha it was a lifelong commitment to world revolution; for Henry it was a lifelong commitment to Natasha.

Their outfits were an identical standard Red Army coat, Russian ushanka fur hat, and desert boots; with, of course, the obligatory array of political badges.[75] The overall look was at one level impressive, aiming to convey a sort of military authority; but in an OG context this was particularly inappropriate. Even in Scotland we have a summer, when temperatures can on some days get up to 20 centigrade or even beyond. Natashen were kitted out to survive a Siberian winter. Natasha could carry off anything, but poor Henry sometimes sweated in a most uncomfortable manner.

I once squeezed into their Trabant car on a very hot day in July to travel the long distance to a game in Aberdeenshire. Both of them were kitted out in normal style, and reflective of the quality of communist East Germany's prized vehicle, the windows didn't open. It was a very long and ripe trip, with the main musical accompaniment a very old tape of Soviet fighting songs. After the game, I made up an excuse that I was staying in Aberdeen to visit relatives and returned home by train.

---

[75] Badges were very common amongst leftie people in the 1980s. Many of these were because we used to 'Rock Against' lots of things – Thatcher, the Tories in general, fascism, apartheid, homophobia, etc. It was generally well intentioned, but not always entirely true. I once went to a 'Rock against the right wing' fundraising night where the only music available was a collection of Burt Bacharach records.

For some reason, East Germany seemed more the apple of Natashen's eyes than the Soviet Union. They regularly holidayed there in an industrial town. Their holiday snaps – normally near a statue of 'comrades fallen fighting fascism' – suggested their 'resort' appeared to emulate the less affluent areas of Middlesbrough.

The most extreme form of this adoration happened one summer, when we noticed gradual changes in Henry's appearance. He started to look older, wore heavy-rimmed spectacles, and in a matter of weeks had developed greying sideburns. We became concerned for his health, and a subsequent enquiry produced an extraordinary response: 'No I'm fine, I am just trying to look a bit more like Erich Honecker.'

It turned out this was Natashen's poster boy – the leader of the German Democratic Republic's Communist Party. It certainly wasn't for aesthetic reasons; Erich looked like a slightly sinister Jobcentre advisor. But just as the ridicule from Henry's statement was about to begin, he added with a lecherous smile, 'The look really seems to do things for Natasha.' We had perhaps underestimated his ploy, and within weeks, at least four other OGs were sporting eyewear quickly labelled as 'Honeckers'.

Henry Sherwood's lifestyle raised the age-old question, 'Can you keep politics out of sport?' In his case the answer was definitely 'no'. On one occasion Henry's political convictions won us a game, but twice they contributed to our defeat.

The day 'Stalinism' won a match for the OGs came first. Batting second in an important cup game, we were really up against it when Henry joined me at the wicket. We had lost five of our best batsmen, and Henry and I were now the only hope. At our mid-wicket chat, as the established batsman, I led the conversation with my characteristically positive outlook: 'Guess we're fucked here.' Henry appeared initially to accept this, but then looked up and saw the bowler. He visibly angered. 'That bastard is the big polisman that nicked me on a CND rally last month!' He walked away deep in thought, and then wandered back and announced loudly to the bewildered bowler, who clearly had no recollection of Henry: 'Stalingrad, comrade, Stalingrad!'

It was a reference to the decisive battle of the Second World War, when in late 1941 the Red Army were close to defeat and pegged back to the city of Stalingrad on the Volga river. In a heroic defence over many months, the Russians held firm, finally gained the ascendancy, and drove the attacking Nazis back. Though it took a while, history suggests this battle signalled that Germany would ultimately lose the war.

Henry had convinced himself, and then, bizarrely, me, that our struggle in Kilmacolm that day was the equivalent of defeating 'the fascist oppressors', as represented by the bowler, PC Plod. After every over, as we clawed our way back into the game, Henry approached me with the constant refrain, 'We owe it to the heroic defenders. We cannot let them down.' Eventually, through Henry's greatest ever innings, we won the game. Though not perhaps with the same significance as the battle, it felt great. We returned to our victorious dressing room both whistling the Soviet Union national anthem.

But Henry's politics also had adverse sporting consequences. Once, on the way to an evening league game, carrying him and our best bowler, Henry's Trabant broke down on the M8. Refusing to seek help, he vowed to fix this precise piece of East German engineering himself. After two hours, he relented and called for assistance. The arriving AA guy condemned the car after 30 seconds, and only reluctantly agreed not to report Henry to the authorities for 'cutting about in that death trap'. Henry and our bowler missed the game, which we narrowly lost.

Stalinism also cost us a cup. One summer, Henry was in the form of his life, and almost singlehandedly got us to the semi-finals of a cup we had never won. In the semi-finals we would face our arch-rivals, Renfrew. It would be a tough match; Renfrew were the strongest team left in the tournament, and we felt sure that victory in the semis would secure us the trophy. With Henry on his current form, we were confident.

The weekend before the match, we were in the pub.

'Good result today. Great knock again Henry; just keep it up and we will pump Babbies in the cup,' commented team skip Jamie Grip.

'Babbies?' questioned Henry.

'Yes Babbies – Renfrew.' I chipped in.

'Why are you calling them Babbies then?' persisted Henry.

'Because they were previously known by their works team name of Babcock and Wilcox. You know, the big manufacturing factory in Renfrew.'

Henry looked concerned. 'This may not be good.' He downed his neat vodka and left.

The next morning, Henry phoned captain Jamie.

'Sorry, I'm out for the semi-final,' he quickly blurted out.

'Why?' responded Jamie, immediately aware of how this affected our chances.

'Natasha, Carlos and I have debated it long into the night. It was quite emotional all round, but in the end I – as a privileged Old Grammarian – cannot seek to beat a team of workers. It would reinforce historic oppression, and potentially destroy their morale.'

'But Henry,' Jamie pleaded.

He was cut across by Henry before getting any further. 'The decision was taken by committee and is final. I will not be contactable for the rest of the week. No harm meant, but we will be sending a motivational note to Renfrew, hoping for a famous workers' victory.'

Semi-final day arrived, Henry was a no show, and Renfrew won a close contest. After the game, I went into to congratulate them. 'By the way,' I asked, 'how many of you actually work at Babcock's?' After a pause, one of them looked up, and replied, 'Sorry, what's Babcock's?'

But it mattered not – we were out of the cup.

The wound opened up in the OGs over the 'Babbies affair' never really healed. Henry became a less frequent performer, and even more distressingly, Natasha drifted from the scene. Eventually they emigrated to East Germany with Carlos. They were last seen on world television trying to put back broken fragments of the Berlin Wall on the night of ninth November 1989.

Chapter 14 – 'Footballs'

'When they ask who's the fool in the corner crying,
I say, little ole wine drinker me.'

Dean Martin

I am personally to blame for Bob Blackstock's OGs career, which lasted approximately 20 minutes. This is believed to be a club record.

On a family camping holiday in France, sitting outside an adjacent tent I noticed a portly middle-aged man drinking from what looked like a large old-style leather football. He did this from early in the morning to late in the afternoon, as his harassed wife Sandra ferried four young children to and from various holiday activities.

Eventually I approached him, and asked what was in the football-like vessel, which at closer quarters was clearly brown plastic. He was enthusiastic in reply: 'Bob Blackstock.' He offered his hand. 'Five litres of red wine, campsite shop, 10 francs. Not a bad drop.' I computed this to be about 20 pence a litre.

He was, of course, Scottish, and lived in Erskine, only a few miles from the OGs' ground.

Given Bob's routine, we became friendly, and over the remainder of the holiday we shared many a daytime 'football'.

One day he caught me reading a book about cricket. I believe it was the now unlisted 'Quick Runs' by Chris Tavaré[76]. Somewhat surprisingly, Bob said, 'Ah, cricket. Played a bit a school; always quite fancied it.'

Ever keen to curry favour with Frank Uber, I was on it in a flash.

'I play for a team in Kilmacolm, just up the road from you. We're always looking for new recruits.'

'No, I couldn't play. I'd be too old and rubbish,' Bob replied.

---

[76] This is attempted irony. Chris Tavaré was a Kent County and England cricketer of the 1980s. For reaching this level of cricketing excellence he deserves serious respect. But even his closest relatives and friends could never have described his batting as 'exciting', being one of the slowest scorers in recent test match history. Rumours that in later years he transferred his cricket skills to establish an innovative retreat for insomniacs are untrue.

I suspected this was a fairly good assessment, but having read *Death of a Salesman* at school, I worked out a cunning approach: highlight the aspects of the product that you think may best appeal to the target market. Basically, this involved mentioning anything but the actual cricket game.

'Not at all, Bob. You could play for the Sunday team, just friendlies. Great bunch of guys. It's just a laugh and an excuse for a good drink. You'll fit in well.'

My sales trick worked a treat, and two weeks later Bob's 'debut' took place in a home Sunday friendly.

Arriving late as ever, I entered the dressing room and was aggressively informed by Tron that my new recruit 'had not trapped'. I was a bit surprised and went out to see if there was any sign of Bob. I spotted him immediately on the grassy bank on the other side of the field. He lay reposed – lazing in the sun, and dressed in full yellowing old-fashioned whites, with the addition of a pair of well-worn brown brogues. Alongside him sat one of apparently 30 'footballs' (150 litres of wine) he had brought back in his estate car from France. (A wise investment, with even the notional cover price of £30 reduced for a bulk purchase.)

It was a lovely warm sunny day, and if Bob had been six stones lighter, the scene could have been straight out of *Brideshead Revisited*. Though incredibly, for those familiar with Evelyn Waugh's 1940s Oxford classic, Bob was already too drunk to team up with Sebastian.

'Bob, come and meet the guys,' I shouted over.

'It's OK,' he replied, 'I'm enjoying my wine. 'Want some?' He lifted up his football.

'No, a bit early. I'll let you know when we are ready to start.'

We took to the field having decided to bowl first. I waved for Bob to join us, but he didn't move.

By this time, my teammates were beginning to think Bob was a figment of my imagination, and that I was covering this up by claiming some old drunk on the boundary line was my new recruit.

I went over. 'Time to start, Bob.' He looked at me, and I suddenly saw the subtlety of my Normandy sales pitch backfire.

'You suggested we all just sort of gathered for a drink. You mentioned the actual game so little, I kind of forgot about that bit, and thought it might just be a cover. To be honest, I finished off another one of these in the garage before I left the house.' He raised his football. 'I am in no state to go out there.'

'Come on, Bob, you're making me look a bit foolish here. Give it a go.'

'OK then.' He staggered to his feet, and I directed him to field at third man.[77]

The game started, and as hoped, the ball went nowhere near Bob. He was all but forgotten about until the start of the fifth over about 15 minutes later, when a thick edge made its way to Bob. 'Keep it to one,' the bowler Tron shouted. It trickled to the boundary for a four. Bob was fast asleep. I ran down to try and salvage the situation, but Tron beat me to it. He poured a bottle of water over a wakening Bob and cried, 'Get him tae fuck!'

I helped a staggering Bob to his car, and, breaking many laws, he managed to drive away.

---

[77] The best fielding position to hide the worst fielder. The ball is hoped to come to this person seldom, and the need to even pretend to try and take a catch is unlikely. On average, OG teams had five players most suited to this position.

The shortest OG career in history was over.

I never saw Bob again, but my wife kept in touch with his wife Sandra for a few months. It transpired that Bob's drinking had become somewhat problematical, building from a very solid foundation in France. Sandra had put her foot down. This had come to a head when, in searing French heat, it was worked out that the logistics of Bob getting his 30 'footballs' into the car at the end of their holiday had necessitated Sandra and her oldest daughter returning to Scotland by bus. Having secured the cheapest travel option based on a circuitous journey via Amsterdam, Bob tried to diffuse the increasingly tense situation.

'I reckon we're still financially up on the deal.' For some reason, this did not work.

'One day's drinking every weekend from now on, or I'm off,' Sandra had warned him when she got back to Erskine 3 days later – noticing that four 'footballs' already lay empty in the kitchen.

'No problem, Saturdays only,' replied Bob. 'From now on I'll be playing cricket every Sunday with that guy Tommy we met on holiday.'

Chapter 15 – Cameos

'All the world's a stage,
And all men and women merely players;
They have their exits and their entrances,
And one man in his time plays many parts.'

William Shakespeare – As You Like it

Given the range of OG characters and incidents, I have found it quite easy to populate these pages – for good or ill. And these are only from my time at the OGs, and my favourite recollections. Older OGs confirm that the club's ability to attract a consistent stream of eccentrics was a feature of its entire 80-year history. I now publicly challenge one of them to write a sister prequel to this volume!

But even from my time, I am conscious of so much that could be written on other OGs. But do they all command a full chapter? An OG cricketing analogy has guided me through this.

Over the years, many OG batsmen were adept at starting an innings well, getting to an OK score, and then doing something ridiculously stupid. In proper cricket this would be recognised as failing to capitalise on a solid base, not applying sufficient concentration, and/or not being very good. But the guilty OG batsmen were uncomfortable with the implied criticism in these explanations. So, they got together and agreed that such innings were to be more positively known as 'cameos'. These were short and good to watch performances of some value which highlighted the batsmen's promise - but not considered match winning contributions.

Transferring this logic, the following OGs are given 'cameo' roles in this volume.

Lloyd Harrods

A truly unacceptable figure, Lloyd was an ageing sexually deviant wicket keeper, who pedalled Viagra in the dressing room before it was officially patented. 'Hard as a stump and longer in the ground,' was a particularly choice selling line. As some sort of defence, Lloyd had clearly had a difficult marriage. He once revealed that he had to finally accept the relationship was over when his wife gave him vouchers for a local prostitute as a Christmas gift. It was their first married yuletide.

Lloyd was a taxi driver by occupation, and he regaled us with many tales of apparent sexual conquest by asking any single woman getting into his cab if they played any sports, and then immediately having to hand in the door pocket the appropriate ball used – tennis, hockey, golf, and even a shuttlecock. 'Works every time!' Lloyd claimed.

Given his shrivelled and ageing frame, and general unpleasantness, this appeared unlikely. Lloyd was not asked to many dinner parties. He was also a complete chancer.

About five years after the OGs folded and I had decommissioned my whites, Lloyd phoned me on a late August night.

'Hi Tommy, how are things?' he opened.

'Who is this?' I replied.

'Lloyd...Lloyd Harrods from the cricket. Remember those blue pills I gave you?'

I quickly interrupted. 'Yes of course. How are you. Still got the taxi?'

This was really the only other thing I knew about him. He knew even less about me. So, the next part was tricky.

'How's that eh...stuff you do?' Lloyd continued.

'You mean my job? Yes, it's good.'

'And you and Lou still OK?'

'Yes, my wife Sue is fine.'

Lloyd had run out of chit-chat. It was the longest conversation I had ever had with him.

'Did you want anything in particular, Lloyd?'

'Well now you ask, what you up to at the weekend?'

'Nothing much.'

Now, I was much too old to have said something as blatantly stupid as this. But I had.

'Well as you might know, I am still playing with the Glasgow University staff team.[78] Due to a combination of bad luck, injuries and deaths, we've had a pretty indifferent season. The last game is on Saturday. If we lose, we'll finish bottom and be relegated.'

---

[78] It is a curious thing in club cricket, but people can end up playing for staff teams of institutions they couldn't get into, work teams where they have never worked, and as former pupils of schools they were unaware existed.

Sadly, I now realised where this call was headed.

'We really need to shore up the middle order batting, and I immediately thought of you.' I later found out I was the fifth OG he had called.

Foolishly, I eventually agreed.

Come the Saturday, I had managed to put together some sort of cricket kit, and headed off to the ground in the west of Glasgow. I was feeling nostalgic and mellow. My vision of the day was to do very little in terms of cricket, bat down the order, and generally wander about dispensing avuncular advice to my young teammates.

As I entered the dressing room, I immediately required to reappraise. I appeared to have entered a holding pen for veterans on Armistice Day before they walked down Whitehall. Approaching 50, I was the youngest by a good 15 years.

Recovering, another thought hit me.

'Lloyd not here yet?'

'No, no,' a very well-spoken teammate, who was either close to 80 or had experienced some very tough times, replied.

'That young rascal [Lloyd was at least 60] has chosen to miss this crucial game. He has wooed a young lady whom he met whilst chauffeuring [taxi driving], and has persuaded her to join him for a cultural weekend in Hartlepool.'

Though stunned, I analysed these two sentences, and reflected how differently an OG such as Tron may have articulated the core information they contained.

'So, he's not playing?'

'Indeed no. But true to his word, he said he would source a youthful replacement who could run around like a whippet in the field for us.'

'Welcome, Tommy,' said another of the dons. This led to a general appreciative rattling of sticks.

After the toss, the captain returned.

'We're batting,' he announced. 'Tommy, if you would be good enough to take up the number 11 berth, I'd be very grateful. Got to keep you fresh for all that fielding.'

Fortunately, the game lasted about 10 minutes and was then rained off.[79]

By a quirk of how points and percentages are allocated in cricket, this actually meant the university staff avoided relegation. I cannot begin to imagine the team that finished below them.

Doctor Dick Bap

Dick continues the academic theme. He was a senior lecturer in forensic science at the University of Strathclyde, and the double of the 1960s and 70s comic actor Derek Nimmo. A spinner with a record of never bouncing the ball on the pitch, he nevertheless remained overwhelmingly and relentlessly positive.

Famously, after a talented young left-hand batsman had deposited him 30 yards over the boundary and into a nearby garden for three consecutive sixes, he announced with all sincerity, 'He's falling into my trap. Maybe drop another man back.' It was the quickest hundred ever scored against the OGs.

---

[79] Cricket is a long game and Scottish summers are short. Consequently, the scope to replay weather affected games is limited.

Dick had a consistently odd way of congratulating teammates who had done well. Not for him a simple 'well batted' or 'well bowled'. Rather he would quietly sidle up alongside you, place his arm on your shoulder, and whisper, 'Capital fellow.' It was strangely motivating.

Dick also claimed to have Dodi Fayed's shirt in his freezer – a reference to the university's ongoing role in the investigation of the car crash that killed Dodi and Princess Diana.

Dick is one of a long line of itinerant and eccentric academics who played for the OGs. A further dedicated volume of chronicles would be needed to do them all justice.

Arthur French

A long-standing OG slow bowler, famous for looking exactly the same at about 40 from the day he joined the OGs at 16 to the day he retired in his mid-60s. Softly spoken and dryly humorous, he was a modest player who had an uncanny knack of getting the opposition professional (i.e. best/only player) out. This was always with his 'straight one'.

This requires a little technical explanation. Slow bowlers are normally expected to spin the ball.

This involves releasing the ball in such a way that it spins awkwardly when it bounces and hits the seam. Good spinners – with none better in the history of the game than the Australian legend Shane Warne – are very difficult to bat against. They also cleverly vary their bowling, by sometimes *not* spinning a ball – known as a 'straight one'. If the batsman anticipates this ball will spin, he can often be in trouble.

It is generally accepted that Arthur French wasn't quite as good as Shane Warne. Every ball he bowled was a 'straight one', as he was incapable of spinning the ball. This complete lack of ability could bamboozle good batsmen, and thinking that by the law of averages Arthur must spin one ball at some point, they would play a stupid shot and get out.

Arthur's ability to regularly achieve this outcome over the years is extraordinary. Evan Tron claims that in 48 years of playing for the OGs, Arthur took a total of 170 wickets (just under four per season, including six 'clean sheets'), and that 55% of these were professionals.[80]

In his personal life, Arthur had a unique way of keeping trim, once claiming he had never eaten anything but breakfast cereal since his early 20s. He

---

[80] Arthur French strongly denies these statistics, and has on more than one occasion threatened legal action.

also seemed to have an off-field wardrobe that consisted entirely of saffron-coloured polo shirts.

Boris Lost

Boris was a legendary council-employed groundsman. He spoke and comported himself as if he had come from a monied background that had all gone wrong.

But by the time of his involvement with the OGs, Renfrew District Council had at least ensured he did once again have an – albeit small – 'pot to piss in'.

English, and with an outrageous but charming stutter, after a few years of wicket cutting, Boris asked if he could maybe get a game. Being from a country that played 'serious' cricket, Frank Uber immediately recruited him.

We had great hopes, slightly dampened by him turning up at his debut already fully kitted out in a blazer, old-style whites which were more accurately a light mustard colour, and a Paisley-patterned cravat. This reflected Boris's general sartorial approach, best explained by his family's official census categorisation as 'fading gentry'.

I first met him, having been 'drawn'[81] to share a room with him on our annual tour of Dumfries. Late on arrival at our hotel, I was told Boris had already arrived. I decided to quickly dump my bag in the room before heading back down for a pint. As I pushed open the door, it immediately hit a solid object. 'One moment,' Boris replied from inside. After a few seconds of noise, the door finally fully opened.

"T. D. Smart, I presume?' asked Boris extending his hand. He was dressed only in a pair of silk maroon boxer shorts and gartered bright yellow socks.

'Sorry about that,' he continued. 'Just ironing my smoking jacket and slacks for tonight's festivities.' He pointed to a now relocated ironing board on the far side of the room.

The same trip also provided some explanation for Boris's clearly fragile financial situation.

Awakening in a shaky condition, I looked across to find Boris's bed empty and meticulously made up. For some reason, it reminded me of a hospital visit to an old dying friend. You turn up at

---

[81] It was never made clear when this 'draw' actually took place. I was certainly not present.

the ward without notice, look at the empty bed and sigh, 'It was for the best. Rest in peace, mate.'

With seconds to spare, I made it to breakfast. Most of my teammates were already there, but not looking in the best shape for the sporting challenge ahead.

'No Boris?' asked Craig Thomas.

'I assumed he was down already; he'd clearly gone from the room sometime before I woke up.'

We broke our fast sedately – a technically questionable statement as the last eight men standing had ordered 'chips for twenty' at 5am from room service. Little more was said of Boris.

Just when we were about to leave, he appeared holding two large shopping bags. He then raised these aloft. 'The early b-bird boys, the early b-bird,' he shouted triumphantly.

Like an excited schoolboy, he then began to spread his wares on the table. It was truly the biggest lot of dated shite imaginable, made worse by the fact some items came in multi-packs. Highlights included ex-World War II batteries, three Binatone radios, a vastly out-of-date catering pack of pilchards, an unreleased dinner plate celebrating Edward VIII's ten years on the throne (appropriately in German), a dusty bottle of Welsh mead, and his pièce de résistance, a 'solid gold' Vietnamese lighter.

'What a cracking wee market, and surprisingly quiet. N-negotiated the lot for just £200. But n-no point in any of you heading round, as I was the o-only person left; it was closing up. The market guys were in g-great humour as I waved them goodbye.'

'Good job I headed up early last night after R-red Can was sick on my jacket. Every cloud, eh?' Boris completed his update.

No-one could really speak. Some of us just passed round Boris's loot, trying desperately not to laugh. Eventually, the silence was broken by Donald Track. 'I need a fag. Mind if I borrow the Vietnamese lighter?'

'No p-problem D-donald - but look after it. I'm hoping to sell it on a for a f-fortune when I get back to G-Glasgow.'

Donald quickly returned asking a nearby waiter, 'Do you sell matches?'

Given the entertainment he had provided, later that day Boris was allowed one of his few cricketing outings for the OGs. This again highlighted that, in a very competitive field, Boris was by some margin the worst cricketer in OG history. The following AGM unanimously passed a motion that, in the event Boris was ever the only 11th man option, we would simply play with 10.

Boris's favourite song was 'Burlington Bertie from Bow' (unfortunate indeed, given his stutter), which he would recite repeatedly whilst rolling the wicket. He was also known to mention that on a sunny day, our cricket ground reminded him of a famous scene in *The Sound of Music*.   This perhaps explains his obsession with Dame Julie Andrews and what later happened to him - as summarised in Chapter 17.

Dawid Biro

Dawid was a white West Indian, but he shared only one cricketing characteristic from that oasis of genius: he had fabulous cricket voice. Deep, resonant and informed, with your eyes closed in conversation you could be listening to 'whispering death' himself – Michael Holding.

Michael was another of that world-conquering Caribbean team of the 1980s. One of the best and quickest bowlers of all time, he went on to an outstanding career as a commentator. But the comparison between Dawid and Michael ended at their similar voices. Sadly, Michael's voice did not win cricket games. Dawid's actual cricketing ability was much more OG standard. And at the lower end.

It also transpired Dawid's involvement with the OGs may have had an ulterior motive. We worked out at the subsequent Christmas get-together that across the season, he had weekly singled one of us out to generate interest in what was clearly a Ponsi scheme. His approach was formulaic, aided by his ever-impressive tone.

'No harm to the rest of the guys, but I can see you've got a bit more about you. I've got something I may be able to let you in on. It only needs a few quid up front.'

Predictably, only one OG took the bait: Denzil. The conversation between these two giants of international finance as they tried to defraud each other was sadly not recorded for posterity. If it had been, it would surely still form the basis of a learning workshop at annual Davos summits.

Tron also suggested Dawid and his wife Creole were trying to get a swingers scene going at the club. This was never proven. Given the source of the rumour, it may have been wishful thinking; sizeable Creole was, as they say, 'all woman'.

The man with no arse

This was actually an opponent of the OGs but given his albeit brief impact on our history, he merits a place in these chronicles. I cannot remember who he played for, and he appeared only to be in our league for one season. This suggests he may have been an itinerant worker who relocated.

Bowling first, we were well on top one Saturday league game after taking a lot of early wickets. Normally at this level, if you got the top four or five batsmen out, the rest of the players were poor, and the innings was quickly over. Out to bat shuffled a tall and very thin man. Frankly, he did not look like a cricketer. In technical parlance, he had every appearance of a 'walking wicket'. All our bowlers wanted to bowl at him to improve their individual performances.

Jim Track had first go. But the normally reliable Jim lost all sense of direction. Wide followed wide down the leg side, and the 'better' balls were easy to hit as they were also badly misdirected. Next up to bowl for us, burly Jamie Grip. Again, without explanation, the same thing happened. Wides and easy runs. By this time, our opponent, who was self-evidently a very limited player, had made over 20.

'Give me the ball,' I demanded. 'One good delivery and this pantomime is over.'

Though generally more wayward and adventurous than Jim and Jamie, I did not think I could do any worse than what I had recently witnessed. But worse I was; I simply could not land the ball anywhere near where I meant to. This pattern continued with all our bowling options. Our shilpit adversary ended with 75 runs, having eventually run out of partners. It was a match-changing performance.

As we sat defeated and puzzled in the dressing room, one question reverberated: 'How could such a poor batsman have got all these runs and cost us victory?' Suddenly, and with solemn importance, Trevor Stone spoke:

'I think I have it, gents,' he opined. 'The problem is that that guy has absolutely no arse'.

Stunned silence.

'As I see it,' continued Trevor, 'all our bowlers subconsciously take their aim by calculating where the batsman's arse is. Given the lack of this reference point, and an unawareness of this fact, collectively our bowling attack was unable to recalibrate.'

'Absolute shite!' our bowlers cried in unison.

The issue was disregarded, and the normally respected Trevor was ridiculed for weeks thereafter.

In the return match towards the end of the season, our bowlers had another shocker. The man with no arse scored an unbeaten century. Despite being again on the losing side, Trevor Stone smirked all night through his post-match pints.

The reason the man with no arse never returned for another season only became known a few years later. After some false starts, donor-based reconstructive surgery was successful – in fact, very successful. He was subsequently spotted and head hunted by a London-based agency, and went on to model a well-known brand of jeans.

PART 3 -
REFLECTIONS AND
THANKS

Chapter 16 – A Bipolar Journey to the History Books

'Only if you have been in the deepest valley, can you ever know how magnificent it is to be on the highest mountain.'

Richard Milhous Nixon[82]

Anyone who has played any form of amateur team sport will, I suspect, reflect on the days when they were world beaters, and the days they appeared unable to recognisably recreate the basic premise of the game. In a way, this disparity is probably what keeps us coming back.

It is not about simply winning and losing, which everyone experiences. It is much more primal. Generally, I liked to win, but was never too down in defeat. This, I suspect, is one of the hundred reasons

---

[82] You do not have to like someone to quote them. For example, I have always thought Hitler's observation that 'These big sturdy black boots are just the job for a Russian winter' was very apt. Pity he never supplied any to his troops.

why Ian Botham is one of the greatest players of the modern era, and I am not.

But there is a different spectrum: the serious highs and the desperate lows. I would argue the OGs would have perhaps been much closer to international recognition if the *range* in this spectrum was the benchmark.

Let's start with the high end: what I conclude is the second most important moment in OG history.

At the level the OGs played, most games were in a regional league around Glasgow. Complementary cup competitions were based on a similar geography. But in the early 1980s, the OGs took a huge leap and entered the Scotland-wide Small Clubs Cup.[83]

This was serious stuff. It moved us beyond our local patch, where you knew all of the teams and the core of the guys who played for them.

When the Small Clubs Cup was drawn, it was a whole new world. Unless it was geographically obvious by the name, you didn't necessarily know where you were off to in an early away tie. This was both exciting and deflating.

---

[83] Many non-Scottish or cricket loving readers may think this is still only a handful of teams. You'd be surprised: check it out!

One year, we were drawn to travel to the enigmatically and oriental sounding 'Eastern Quarter'. It has to be said that discovering this was on the outskirts of Falkirk was bit of a let-down.

My memory of how we got to the final in 1990 is not that great. But one shrewd observation I can make is that, as a straight knockout format, we could not have lost any games.

For us, the final was a big deal, and, as detailed in Chapter 9, demanded a serious selection meeting; though whether this was of any use is subject to some doubt.

The real enormity of the occasion only hit me when I was told the team bus would pick me up at the end of the road at 10am. A team fucken bus! And this not only carried the eleven chosen warriors, but a twelfth man, Frank Uber, Archie Ranger, Moira, a spattering of former players and – to some annoyance – Bounty.

We arrived at Strathmore's wonderful ground, a little later than anticipated to accommodate 'comfort breaks' for Archie and Tron, who had started their planned day out early. For some reason, Tron was suspended for the final. This is quite an achievement in cricket. I cannot remember the exact reason, but given the player involved it would not have been good.

As we left the bus, we were actually greeted by Scottish Cricket Union officials.

'If any of you guys fancy a net [pre-match practice], we have allocated two to each side,' one of them informed skipper Jamie Grip.

As we watched our opponents practise furiously, and even undertake stretching exercises, our sense of underdog status was truly confirmed.

Losing the toss, we were invited to bat first. After some early nerves, we settled and put up a reasonable score. At the halfway point we were certainly still in the game.

Our bowling performance that day was probably the best cricket played in my time at the OGs. It also reflects an interesting fact which I am sure is very familiar to sport phycologists, irrespective of the sport.

In the lead-up to the game, our research indicated that our opponents had an outstanding batsman called Fraser. He had almost single-handedly guided them to the final through some exceptional performances. It transpired that, despite his name, Fraser was in fact English, and had played at a good level down south. This is the type of English skulduggery all Scots are well aware of.

Despite our anger, and a pathetic attempt at a mid-innings chorus of *Flower of Scotland*, our task remained clear: get Fraser out or lose the cup. But because we had never played our opponents before, none of us knew who Fraser was. Undercover work at the tea break identified an English accent: we had our man.

After quite a few overs, our opponents' response to our score looked frankly uninspiring. On any objective analysis, we were winning. As I fielded on the boundary rope, Tron and Archie did their seventieth circuit of the ground. They were very drunk, but given how much I knew it meant to them, surprisingly smug and calm.

'Looking pretty good,' I said. 'Just got to get Fraser out and we could do this.' For me, Fraser was the English guy who had just come in to bat.

'Fraser's out. You bowled him in the second over.'

'So who's that guy?' I pointed to the batsmen.

'Oh, that's his brother: he's pish,' said Tron. 'Six times in a brothel and still hasn't scored.' For all his faults, Tron did have a good turn of phrase.

Initially, I thought this was just morale building. But as time went on, it did become apparent that the batsmen I thought was 'the real Fraser' would indeed need to have quite a few more visits to a brothel before he would register in the income generation column.

In the end, having got the main man, we won quite comfortably. But it is of some regret to me that the best and most important ball I bowled in my OG career is one I cannot remember. This brings me back to sports psychology: had I known I was bowling at the 'legendary' Fraser, would I still have got him out? To quote a countrywoman of his, 'Am I bovvered?'

This is probably the only time in my sporting life I performed to a support, which probably at its peak grew to approaching 100. Many, many sportsmen and women have regular experience of playing in front of vastly greater numbers. But irrespective of volume, is the pattern the same? As we started as clear underdogs, the encouragement from our supporters was very much of a 'play up and play on' nature – i.e., put up a show, don't make a complete arse of yourself, but ultimately get well beaten. As we began to score a few runs, a subtle change occurred. Still relatively muted, we could hear, 'Come on OGs, we're in this game.'

Then – unbeknown to the players – we dislodged 'the real Fraser'. The volume was considerably upped: 'Come on OGs, this mob are pish!'

Finally, as our opponents crumbled and victory was guaranteed, it then just became a long sustained and full volume, 'OGs! OGs! OGs!' This lasted a full 15 minutes, until the final wicket fell.

The last phase of this lives with me for another reason. Coming from the exceptionally drunk Archie Ranger and Tron, this support was welcome but predictable. But near the end, I also noticed Craig Thomas arm-in-arm, joining in. Craig was an excellent and long-standing OG opener, a bit older than most of us and recently retired. He was a much more reserved character than Archie and Tron, and someone younger OGs always looked up to. He wanted to be out there. It mattered to him, and it mattered to every OG on the pitch.

This victory in terms of simple cricketing achievement was without question our finest hour. And as you hopefully have picked up by now, we knew how to celebrate. I was drunk before leaving the dressing room – not on the basis of huge intakes of alcohol (made up for later), but on adrenalin and tiredness. How much of the aftermath I remember, and how much I was later told about, is a matter of speculation. I think and hope that Frank Uber and Archie Ranger were duly praised; without them, there would have been no OGs.

Another vague memory – subsequently confirmed – was of sitting on the wicket with the entire OG travelling party singing our club song. This was not perhaps the most significant lyrical adaptation in musical history. It consisted of a rendition of the Dean Martin classic, *Little Ole Wine Drinker Me*, but replacing the last line with, 'We are the OGCC'. Whilst never nominated for the Ivor Novello awards, it certainly seemed to work that night.

My final recollection is all this happening whilst some of our number were sporting only jock straps. Denzil (of course), fitness-mad Keith Lochkin, and our 12th man Gordon McLear – no great cricketer, but without question our poster boy. It was homoerotic in nature (a word I discovered 20 years later), and could easily have found its place in an Alan Hollinghurst novel. It may also have lit the candle of the OGs' following of women: but this didn't actually exist.

Three years later, we made the Small Clubs final again. But, as earlier chronicled, we narrowly lost – not entirely, but mainly, because of Denzil. To our credit, we probably partied as hard that night in defeat as in our previous victory. This was only fair as a sporting gesture to our victorious opponents. Given they came from the far north of Scotland and left immediately after the presentations, technically this tribute was *in absentia*. But the opportunity of having a coach with a pre-paid driver was simply too much for the OGs to miss. Why this necessitated a further pitch romp dressed only in jock straps by our three cavaliers from the previous victory, is harder to explain. Particularly as this time they were joined by a similarly attired 20-stone Archie Ranger.

But put to the vote, is the Small Clubs Cup victory in 1990 the most memorable moment in OG history? I suspect not. Returning to the initial premise of this chapter, we now come to objectively the lowest point on our bipolar journey.

France's 'little sparrow', Edith Piaf (reportedly even smaller than Greg Omelette, aka Tonto), once emotionally sang, *'Je Ne Regrette Rien'* – quite an achievement, as she clearly had a pretty shit life.

Later, Scott Walker sang 'No Regrets', which I assume remained true even after he found out he was not in any way related to the other Walker Brothers. Well, I disagree with Edie and Scottie: till the day I die, I will regret not being a part of the fateful OGs XI that crossed the line to take on Crichton Royal in August 1984.

This was a Saturday fun game as the opener in an annual weekend 'tour' to Dumfries. On the Sunday, we played Dumfries CC, a much sterner cricketing challenge. But in an area of Scotland not dense with cricketing options, our Saturday game was against the staff and patients of Crichton Royal Mental Hospital.

Over the years, this became a great day out. Never the most competitive game, it was always played in a good spirit. Some of the guys in Crichton Royal were quite seriously ill, but loved their cricket. Often patients were not distinguishable from the staff. As this was a joke told by a member of staff, I think it is acceptable to recall. Assuming, of course, it was a member of staff.

I had played in the corresponding fixture the previous year to the legendary match, and it was certainly entertaining. Promoted to open the batting, I suspect due to major hangovers in the squad, I played out an uneventful first over. This took about three minutes. In a normal innings of batting, half way through on a warm day (say, after about an hour and a half), 'drinks' would be called. This would tend to involve someone in the batting team coming out with a couple of jugs of orange squash and plastic cups. It was basic, required a break of about five minutes, and was often a great relief after extended endeavour in the sun. It was some surprise, therefore, when the cry of 'Drinks!' went up after the first over. As we looked over, two of our opponents were advancing on the wicket with two hostess trolleys. One contained a high-quality afternoon tea spread of cakes, scones and sandwiches – without crusts! The other carried a full bone china tea set.

Standing there mid-wicket sipping tea and munching a high quality cream scone, was perhaps one of the more unusual experiences in my cricketing career. It was odd after only facing an over, but this placed me in a more rewarding position than my opening partner Donald Track, who had not yet faced a ball.

After about 20 minutes, the game resumed. Donald played out the next over, and I prepared again for strike. 'Drinks!' the cry went up, and the two trolleys once again began to trundle out. Fortunately, a member of staff this time intercepted them, and suggested they leave it a bit.

Such was the fun of a game at Crichton Royal!

Due to the birth of my son, I was not present the following year for the fateful encounter. This was not viewed by the OG authorities as an acceptable excuse for not touring, and I was formally reprimanded at the next AGM.

Cricket is a very uneven game. Though a team sport, at any time it is an individual context of one bowler against one batter. If all 11 in one team are significantly better than the other 11, getting any sort of competitive game is difficult. It is not like, say football, where a poor team can just defend en masse and – although they'll more than likely lose – the game runs its course as some sort of competitive event.[84] Cricket is much more one sided, and games can easily become a joke that neither team enjoys. When, in a friendly, it is apparent that a potential mismatch exists, a 'gentleman's agreement' is that the stronger team bats first. This at least ensures some length of game. Historically, the OGs were much stronger than Crichton Royal, so it was a surprise when our captain advised his teammates that

---

[84] Greenock Morton FC have operated for years on this basis.

Crichton Royal had won the toss and were batting first.

The inevitable happened. After 10 minutes, half of Crichton Royal's batsmen were out. The game looked likely to last about 30 minutes in total. This is frustrating at the best of times; for a team like the OGs on tour, it would have led to a drinking start time of 2pm. This was not advisable.

So Captain Track stood down his proper bowlers, and gave his aspiring second stringers a chance. This would basically 'give' Crichton Royal some sort of score, so that at least a few of our guys had a chance to bat, and we would be out of the pub a little longer. Fortunately, we had in our ranks quite a few second-string bowlers, a couple of third stringers, and a solid cadre of fourth stringers. But despite some of the worst bowling imaginable, Crichton Royal could only limp to a very poor total of 74. Very easy to reach, we assumed, as their bowlers were no better than their batters.

It is therefore all but impossible to explain a phone call from Dumfries to Frank Uber back in Glasgow later that night.

'How did it go today?' Frank asked.

'Not great.' Trevor Stone had been unluckily identified as our on-site correspondent.

'Tighter than we thought?' asked Frank. 'Probably better to get a good workout before the big test tomorrow.'

'We lost by 69 runs.' Trevor slammed down the phone and headed for the bar.

Hopefully you have done the not so tricky maths. Collectively, the OGs had scored a total of five runs. It is one of the lowest recorded cricket scores of all time.

An even more astonishing conversation was one I had with Jim Track when we met up the following weekend.

'What the fuck?' was, I thought, an appropriate introduction before bursting out laughing.

'To be honest,' said Jim, 'we didn't really do anything wrong.'

'And,' he then added, 'I was second top scorer. I got one.'

There is an old adage in cricket that 'the scorebook doesn't lie'. This is generally true, and though I have often ribbed my colleagues as a non-combatant, initial reports had some validity that on this occasion it did.

Dr. Gordon Bronze opened up the OGs' innings, a big promotion as a lower order batsman, in recognition this would be any easy run chase. He duly crashed the first ball for four. We were cruising to victory. The bowler did not take this well, and turned to the umpire (another Crichton Royal player) and screamed, 'How could you let that happen?'

The umpire looked rattled.

Next ball, our good doctor patted the ball back to the bowler. No run.

'HOWZAAT!' pierced the Dumfries sky.

Up went the dreaded finger. 'Plumb[85], brother,' said the umpire. 'Out.'

In cricket etiquette, the umpire's decision is final. No matter how unfairly treated you feel, off you

---

[85] 'Plumb' means the batter is definitely out leg before wicket (LBW). It is not a hard or controversial decision.

must go. Dr. Bronze headed to the changing room.

In disgust, Jamie Grip went in next, announcing, 'I'm going to get this over with quickly.' As a personal performance, he did. He took an angry swipe, missed the ball and was bowled. Crichton Royal sniffed a chance, particularly after the over ended with a hat trick of leg before wickets, despite one of these being a pleasant shot into the covers, and another being a wide down the leg side.

Four runs, five wickets. Not looking great, but still recoverable.

At this point, skipper Donald Track, one of the men out, approached a Crichton Royal spectator and suggested it was all becoming a bit ridiculous. He immediately said, 'Absolutely, I'll go out and umpire the next over.'

Jim Track was then rapped on the pads and a big appeal went up as he scrambled a single, with the run given to the batsman. Jim later admitted he was probably out.

All seemed back to normal. But by the end of the over, the OGs were all out for five. Three further LBWs and two poor shots of sheer frustration sealed our fate, despite one of the LBW balls apparently ricocheting off a pad for a one bounce four.

The replacement umpire walked off hugging some jubilant Crichton Royal players. 'Unlucky, guys. Just caught us on a good day, I guess,' he said to our stunned ranks. It later transpired he was the hospital's longest-standing patient.

It is an interesting story, but is it true? Other accounts have suggested that whilst the OGs were undoubtedly on the wrong end of some dodgy umpiring, it was also a very poor and undisciplined batting display. A close look at the scorebook from that historic day indicates that this was perhaps the weakest possible OG batting line up in history. Greg Omelette (Tonto),[86] Boris Loss, Denzil, Gavin Bland, and an extremely drunk Archie Ranger.

The explanation for this disaster, that we were playing a team from a mental hospital, has to be subject to serious revision. A handy excuse, but largely inaccurate. What is worse: being all out for five, or then unfairly blaming this on the mental health of your opponents?

Nonetheless, as time passed, becoming one of the famous 'Crichton Royal brigade' became an

---

[86] A cricketing joke only. Tonto was a very small chap: he once missed half a season to injury after ducking into a Yorker.

almost exclusive clique within the OGs. How *not* being a part of a team bowled out for five became an implied criticism, is difficult to fathom. But this was the OGs. I reckon about four people who played at Crichton Royal that day also won the Small Clubs Cup. I would never risk asking them which 'achievement' made them more proud. The likely answer scares me.

And of course, in typical OG style, the same touring squad then chased down 225 against a good Dumfries side the next day, for a thrilling two wicket victory.

Chapter 17 – Whither the OGs?

'It is difficult to make predictions, especially about the future.'

Danish proverb

The tales chronicled above took place 30 years ago. The OGs, with recruitment problems continuing and an ever-creaking squad, limped on, but eventually folded at the start of the 21st century. The final blow was when Frank Uber – a lifelong devotee of Napoleon Bonaparte – decided to spend the late autumn of his days on the Italian island of Elba.

As reflected upon further in the final chapter, relationships in cricket can be unusual. Although I would consider many of my former teammates to be good friends, ultimately it was cricket that brought us, and kept us, together. When the end came, we largely drifted apart, regrouping infrequently at events such as Archie Ranger's funeral. At one level, this is helpful to these memoirs as I can only speculate (i.e. make up) what happened next to the key characters.

Frank Uber retired from his job as a Linwood undertaker, and as mentioned, settled on the island of Elba. It has to be said that this was his second choice, having discovered that Ryanair did not fly direct to St. Helena. On Elba, he wrote a critically acclaimed introduction to a new edition of Dale Carnegie's classic, *How to Win Friends and Influence People*. Following a massive publicity campaign, Sir Frank Uber was awarded a long overdue knighthood for services to cricket in 2010.

Archie Ranger discovered there was an afterlife, and that it was well supplied with gin. He is now a powerful lead singer in a heavenly choir, and the club formerly known as Rangers have now won a major trophy. But this is less important, as following an extensive programme of re-education, Archie became a Roman Catholic six years after his death. He still has a soft spot for the Gers, but now when he watches an Old Firm game, he just wants to see the better team win. In his will, Archie bequeathed his house to Ralston Bowling Club, and his drinks trolley to Jim Track. Jim reports that, after a sustained effort, he finally finished its contents in late 2019.

Little is known for certain of Yogi's post-OG life. Shortly after the OGs folded, it is rumoured he hurriedly left the UK. A forthcoming book is currently in preparation suggesting he was indeed the 'fifth man', alongside Burgess, Philby, Maclean, and Blunt. This is on hold for libel reasons until formal confirmation of his death is received. In 2018, British intelligence identified a strange bear-like figure over Vladimir Putin's shoulder at a Moscow May Day parade. On closer analysis, it became clear this was not a model of Russia's animal emblem, but human.

Married a rumoured nine times, it is now understood this was not because of Yogi's romantic delusions, but as a cover to support a lifelong commitment to undermining the British state. It's now all but certain that he assassinated at least one wife, voluptuous and big-haired Oxana – victim of a pre-planned honeymoon hit. Oxana had finally fallen victim to her lifelong quest to return the Romanovs (of whom she claimed lineage) to the Russian crown.

By way of further important background, it is rumoured Siberian Oxana would have appealed to most heterosexual men. This is thought to explain why Yogi only 'took her out'[87] towards the end of a two-week honeymoon. His handlers in Moscow had instructed him to do this in the taxi back to their hotel after the ceremony. Former cabbie teammate Lloyd Harrods had been temporarily recruited as an accomplice. Unreliable Harrods later claimed he was

---

[87] Apparently, they 'stayed in' quite a lot for the previous 11 days.

involved in some of the subsequent wedding night activities, pithily recalling Oxana as 'uninhibited'.

Despite everything, Moira is understood to still be with Yogi as his true love. They are said to live well in a luxury flat overlooking Red Square with their nine-year-old pup, Twix.

Denzil again confounded his critics.

The forces of the law finally caught up with him at JFK airport, as he fled Britain following his involvement in an international dot.con scandal. Tried in the US, his extradition to the UK failed, and he was sentenced to serve five years in a federal prison. But maintaining his record of luck and bouncing back, Denzil ended up sharing a cell with Jordan Belfort, aka *The Wolf of Wall Street*.

Released from jail, he is now a key partner in Belfort's motivational speaking company and has a rumoured personal fortune of $200 million. He is happily remarried to former sweetheart Susanne, and this arrangement has now been openly consummated. One result is a challenging teenage boy – worryingly called Zeus. He plays golf regularly with Susanne's dad Charlie, who proudly introduces Denzil as 'the son he never had'.

Settled in America, Denzil has refused a number of offers to return to the UK and be nominated as the Tory parliamentary candidate for a safe seat in the south of England. It is not yet clear whether the scale of his historic tax avoidance is large enough to trigger a knighthood.

Of our supporting cast, Jim Track still receives counselling for recurrent nightmares that he is continually frozen on '56 not out'. But he manages to function, and runs a successful ice cream parlour in Largs.

Donald Track retired early from a solid career in the police. With his wife, he now owns a string of care homes in the north of Scotland. Though very much hands on in the business, he has never encountered anything quite as repulsive as Yogi's expulsion at Rolls Royce.

Trevor Stone won £500,000 on *Who Wants To Be a Millionaire?*. He strangely missed out on the full prize by being unable to compose himself to answer the final question, 'What was the middle name of the famous West Indian cricketer Malcolm Marshall?' He now regularly appears on the TV quiz show *Eggheads*.

Jack Donald had an astonishing epiphany in his mid-40s, gave up drinking, and runs an internationally-renowned brand of alcohol-free health retreats. Now looking younger than ever, his favourite film is *The Curious Case of Benjamin Button*.

Jamie Grip manages to write a popular column for the Times Literary Supplement, despite remaining under police surveillance.

Evan Tron gave up on his longer-term hopes to become a merchant sailor. A functioning alcoholic, he works in a joke shop in central Glasgow.

Ritchie Cameron had a successful career as a Procurator Fiscal. But he is now better known under a pseudonym as a famous ballroom dancer, and until recently was a core part of the *Strictly* team.

Mary has had a troubled married life. Gerry gave up joinery and formally joined his father's gangster activities. This has led to a varied and itinerant lifestyle. Her one comfort is endlessly bingeing on repeats of *The Sopranos*. Despite his subsequent wealth, Denzil still owes Mary around £8,000. Gerry is keen to pop over to the States to 'resolve' this, but his father enforces the gangster's code of 'sticking to your own manor'.

Faheed and Wasim gave up the curry business, and now run a very profitable online women's lingerie venture. Transferring learning from previous business experience, their best seller is a lucky dip 'weekend of passion parcel', which retails for a standard £20.

Professor Lionel Degree turned his back on an illustrious academic career, having fallen madly in love with a 16-year-old waiter in an Italian restaurant. Following their civil partnership, they now run a small hotel in the Tuscan hillside village of Barga.

Yuvraj returned to the Punjab. He won four caps for the India B team but failed to break through to the top side. Somewhat surprisingly, he does not mention his cup tie winning eight wickets for nine runs against the OGs in his recent memoir, *My Top 500 Moments in Cricket*.

Sheila Gibb became the successful madame of an upmarket brothel in Bridge of Weir. Although no longer in a relationship, Mike and Sheila are still friends, and he does repairs and odd jobs around the premises after particularly punishing weekends.

Greg Omelette (Tonto) became the most diminutive TV chef in history, and still commands large viewing figures for his iconic food channel show, *Small Plates*. Immediately identifiable by its theme tune of Elton John's *Tiny Dancer*, this low-budget production initially struggled, until the cooking surfaces were lowered and viewers were able to see more than Tonto's forehead.

Boris Lost is currently completing a three-year sentence in HMP Buckley Hall, having been convicted of the persistent stalking of Dame Julie Andrews. His disguise of doing this dressed as a nun enabled him to escape identification for some time. Boris's subsequent court appearance in the same outfit – demanding throughout that he be referred to as Burlington Bertie – did not play out well. Facing an old school judge, this added a year to his sentence.

Stephen Carew abandoned a pedestrian career in retail management. This paid dividends. Retrained, he is now Chief Executive of the Scottish Mortuary Society.

And finally, to the only character in this book immortalised for all time. Bounty died in 1990 as a 15-year-old pup. His brain was donated to veterinary science, and its analysis significantly contributed to new behavioural interventions for wayward dogs. Late identification of a Big Lottery Fund underspend in 2000 led to the commissioning of a bronze statue of Bounty. To her great credit, Sheila Gibb took time off from her demanding brothel duties, squeezed into her yellow polka dot dress, and formally unveiled the statue on a cold and grey April morning in 2001.

Bounty now sits proudly outside the former OG clubhouse in Kilmacolm.

Chapter 18 – Looking back

'That's what they do, these people. They embroider, they improve on the truth – they tell lies.'

Michael Frayn – The Trick of It

If you have got this far, a question I suspect that must have popped into your head is, 'Are these chronicles factually true?' In response, I require to fall back on the artistic concept of 'the beholder's share'. With apologies to anyone that actually knows about this stuff, I would summarise as follows.

No work of art – picture, music, book, sculpture, etc. – exists independently in its own right. The key 'moment of art' is every individual person's experience of this: the viewer, the reader, the listener. As everyone comes with their own baggage, taste, history, etc., then everyone's experience is different. This is irrespective of the fact that the actual piece of art has objectively not changed.

This is getting too complicated, for me at least. So, I'll try again.

I find listening to Celine Dion's music excruciating. I would rather clean Yogi's pants. But some people – incredibly – like her. The songs they hear are, however, the same. Setting aside that those who like this music are wrong and unwell, their 'beholder's share' is clearly different to mine, which would be better described as 'beholder's pain'.

In short, people see and experience things differently.

So, any readers of this book can experience it as they choose. If it being true works for you, fine; if you think it is complete fiction, that is also fine. Draw your own conclusions, though as a slight hint, scepticism may be the best starting point.

Any more scholarly attempt to determine the overall factual authenticity of these tales could perhaps learn from an approach pioneered by Historic Environment Scotland. This organisation owns and maintains many magnificent properties in Scotland, and tells the nation's story in a range of exciting and innovative ways. My personal favourite is Neolithic Orkney, a range of sites centred on the discovery of the settlement of Skara Brae.

I would strongly encourage all readers to visit Skara Brae – it is fascinating. But try and do it when the unbearable and largely American cruise ship hordes are not in Orkney. They swamp the site asking inane questions, thinking 'old' means the 18th century TV drama, *Outlander*. They are only about 7,000 years out. This may provide some insight as to why these people once elected Donald Trump. If you visit, and happen to see any 'cruisers', just shoot them.[88]

Skara Brae is seriously old stuff – even older than Alf Gibbs and Dougie Caper in the twilight of their OG careers. Discovered in the late 19th century, a storm unearthed a settlement from 5,000 BC that upset all previous estimates of when humans first came together in Europe and lived in communities. This is historically fascinating, but challenging. How do we begin to try and understand everything from the limited evidence we have from so far in the past?

The Skara Brae visitor centre approaches this in a clever and honest way. Information is provided in

---

[88] It is impossible to visit Skara Brae and not end up with a head full of thoughts and questions. For work research, I recently asked a very knowledgeable site guide what the most recurrent questions were that she was asked by 'cruisers'. First was how tall the people were, kind of odd but OK. Second was the utterly irrelevant, 'Have you ever met any of the cast of Outlander?' And, perhaps inevitably, the third was, 'Do you know if there is a McDonalds in Kirkwall?" (Orkney's main town.) Land of the free, I salute you! Though for clarity and correctness, I do not actually mean for you to shoot them.

three categories. What we definitely know; what we think we know; and what we can only speculate about. The best example of the last of these, is why this relatively sophisticated community disbanded, and humans only appeared to come together again in this way thousands of years later.[89]

I think paraphrasing the Skara Brae approach may be the best way to reflect on these memoirs: some of them are true; some of them might be true; and some are completely made up.[90] But given the dominance of categories two and three, I thought I should finish up with some comments that are 100% true.

In writing my memories, I have more than confirmed to myself that the time I spent playing for the OGs was a highlight of my life. The cricket itself was great, but all the stuff around it was better – most of all my teammates, their partners, and their animals. This led from the coming together of a hugely diverse group of people who ultimately had one consistent thing in common – a love of cricket. In terms of occupation, interests, class, politics, race,

---

[89] One explanation may neatly return us to the coronavirus origins of this book.

[90] Libel lawyers take note: anything you have been approached about is firmly in the third category.

and football allegiances, we covered the whole spectrum.

There were also lots of very basic things I never knew about many of the people I played with for years; for example, what they did, where they lived, and whether they cross dressed in the close season. These things simply didn't matter; we never ran out of conversation, so irrelevant domestic detail seldom made it on to the agenda.

The nature of cricket also creates unusual relationships. From early May to late August, you can spend more time with cricket colleagues than members of your close family (the reason some OGs were so keen on the game): all day Saturday and Sunday, and two weekday nights. But then, other than a Christmas night out and a drunken AGM, you do not see them at all between September and April. Even though some of us went to support St. Mirren, we never tended to go as a group, having other social circles for this. In a way it is a bizarre type of friendship, but it worked. Though always enjoying their company, I had no great desire to see cricket friends in the long Scottish winter. In writing this, however, I only now reflect that there may well have been a strong winter social calendar I was just not made aware of!

Very late in my tales, I have to admit that unlike many of the folks in these chronicles, I was not a 'one club man'. In my formative years, I played at a so-called 'higher level' (these things are all relative). When I moved to the OGs to join my pals, some people thought it was a strange decision. In a life of many mistakes, this was not one.

Writing this book has also reaffirmed my love of the game of cricket. I find it hard to imagine my life without it. I will have succeeded beyond my dreams if you have stayed with this book, but still don't get this. Please give cricket a go – watching if not playing. Would it be possible to create better theatre than the 2019 Cricket World Cup final?

But this, of course, is only one of a number of cricket 'formats'. I think this adds to the confusion for non-believers, and perhaps reduces their ease of access to the great game. As a simple guide, despite many historic failures to explain this, I will nevertheless try again.

The longest form of the game is a Test Match. This can last for up to five days and is only played at international level. The other 'long' form of the game in England is a County Championship match. (Most other countries have their equivalents.) This can last up to four days, though in my younger days, it was three. Then we have a 'one day game' (50 overs per team). This can be international or domestic, and can last up to eight hours. Finally, we have the more recently introduced 'pup' – Twenty20 cricket. With 20 overs a side, this lasts about four hours and is commonly played in the late afternoon or evening.

So, which is best? Amongst cricket buffs this is an endless and unresolvable argument. Everyone has their own preferences and prejudices. I think one way to work through this is to think of cricket formats like relationships, and in my description below I reveal my own viewpoint.

A five-day Test Match is like a long, happy marriage. It may start as a slow burner, but once the penny drops, it is rewarding like no other scenario. The real deal – true love!

A four-day county match is like a long, bland marriage. It has its moments, certainties and longevity; but can be a bit dull, and people sometimes only stick with it through familiarity.

A one-day match is like a reasonable length relationship that runs its course. Enjoyable and satisfying in many ways, it does the job. But after you experience a Test Match, you become aware of its limitations.

A Twenty20 match is a one-night stand: exciting, exhilarating, short lived, and ultimately meaningless.

Very recently, even shorter forms have been introduced, such as 'The Hundred', and 10 over-a-side matches. I guess to extend the analogy, these need to be viewed as a 'quickie' in a toilet or a broom cupboard.

The analogy of cricket formats and relationships gets on to trickier ice when considering which option is for you. In cricket, many people will harmlessly and simultaneously indulge in the full menu. In relationships, whilst this strategy is not unknown, it is problematic and harder to condone.

So, you will see I have declared my preference on cricket formats. The longer form of the game – a five-day Test Match – is perhaps a harder thing to immediately love, but you are watching a living organism. Everything and nothing is happening. The pitch, the ball and the weather are constantly changing and influencing the outcome of the game; and like life itself, though you think it might be, it is never standing still. Though apparently going on a bit, a few key moments can determine everything that follows.

Allow me this final indulgence, please. I can only repeat: go to a big cricket game, ideally picking a glorious summer's day in June at Lords. It is visually stunning, and the atmosphere is like calm electricity. The crowd is a random cross section of age, class, ethnicity, and gender. As an added bonus, you can observe and/or participate in thousands of people getting collectively drunk as the day progresses. Cricket nut Stephen Fry once said he envied people who had never read a P.G. Wodehouse novel because, unlike him, they had it all ahead of them. If you have not yet been to a cricket match in the sun, I am similarly envious.

My first game watching English county cricket has some strong personal memories. In the early summer of 1976, my father died suddenly when I was 14 years old.[91] It was a very strange summer, which I still largely recall as a sort of haze. The weather was inappropriately glorious. In August, my mum took me and my two brothers to friends in Chatham, Kent, to attempt some form of holiday.

I watched all three days of a county match between Kent and Gloucestershire at the famous county ground in Canterbury. I was lucky and saw the

---

[91] My father – John (Jack) Smart – was the last ever Provost of Paisley.
Perhaps another reason why I am so prejudiced in favour of my home town.

great Pakistani and Gloucestershire batsmen Zaheer Abbas score 200 in the first innings and 100 in the second. He was not out both times. It seemed graceful and effortless, and made up my mind that I wanted to be more of a batter than a bowler – as, on that day, did all the Kent bowlers! Zaheer did it all wearing glasses, which for some reason I thought was just wonderful.

But for me, it was not Zaheer's fabulous achievement that make these days at Canterbury so important. Rather, it is my memory of being on my own, which can't be right – my brothers must have been there, and an adult must have driven us to the ground. But I was 'in the zone'; it was just me and Zaheer. At some point watching him bat, I felt sort of normal for the first time in that dreadful summer, and realised that life would go on and be OK. Thank you, Zaheer Abbas, and cricket.

To conclude: the draft of the chapter I wrote on cricket and writers provoked more hostile reaction than any another. Highlight feedback included 'Pretentious wanker', in a style of discourse redolent of how Scottish men speak to their close friends.

In the same spirit I respond, 'Fuck you,' and maintaining my pretensions, unrepentantly end with a quote from F. Scott Fitzgerald as he declared The

Great Gatsby's innings. I believe this appropriately concludes my tales and confirms my friends' shallowness:

'So we beat on, boats against the current, borne back ceaselessly into the past.'

Acknowledgements and thanks

All my real OG teammates.

The magnificent and irreplaceable game of cricket.

Covid 19 – for the collapse of my business. (Obviously there were some downsides.)

Sir Vivian Richards, Sachin Tendulkar, Bob Willis, Malcolm Marshall, Michael Holding, and Shane Warne - for being brilliant inspirational cricketers, and a bit more.

Zaheer Abbas – for helping a wee Scottish guy at a difficult time.

John Locke, Thomas Hobbes, John Rawls, and Niccolo Machiavelli – for introducing me to literature.

Curry, and the great curry houses of the Glasgow area.

Renfrew Cricket Club (Babbies) – for providing a wholly exaggerated and unfair representation as unpopular OG rivals.

The heroic workers of East Kilbride Rolls Royce.

Tory politicians – every book needs baddies.

Tess of the d'Urbervilles, Emma Bovary, and Dorothea Casaubon – for what might have been.

Francis Scott Fitzgerald – for *The Great Gatsby*, and saving the world from my writing (until now).

Paisley St. Mirren Football Club – for everything, and all that's still to come.

Wee Ginge (my wife) - for telling me to piss off and leave her alone.

Bounty.

THE END

Printed in Great Britain
by Amazon